rio de janeiro

second edition

Excerpted from *Fodor's Brazil*

fodor's travel publications
new york • toronto • london • sydney • auckland
www.fodors.com

contents

maps

on the road with fodor's

THE MORE YOU KNOW BEFORE YOU GO, the better your trip will be. The city's most fascinating small museum or its best beach could be just around the corner from your hotel, but if you don't know it's there, it might as well be across the globe. That's where this guidebook and our Web site, Fodors.com, come in. Our editors work hard to give you useful, on-target information. Their efforts begin with finding the best contributors—people with good judgment and broad travel experience—the people you'd poll for tips yourself if you knew them.

Joyce Dalton, who contributed to Practical Information, has been traveling for more years than she cares to count. Her travel articles and photos appear in numerous trade and consumer publications.

Denise Garcia is a journalist and has traveled to and lived in various places around the world. She put her talents to work on Practical Information from her home in Rio de Janeiro.

Compulsive traveler and Rio native **Ana Lúcia do Vale,** who updated all the Rio content, is a journalist whose career has included producing and directing Brazilian television shows as well as work with a news agency and writing for the *carioca* newspaper *O Dia*.

Don't Forget to Write

Keeping a travel guide fresh and up-to-date is a big job. So we love your feedback—positive and negative—and follow up on all suggestions. Contact the Pocket Rio de Janeiro editor at editors@fodors.com or c/o Fodor's, 280 Park Avenue, New York, New York 10017. And have a wonderful trip!

Karen Cure
Editorial Director

COLOMBIA
Boa Vista
RORAIMA
Rio Branco
BR 174
Rio Negro
Anavilhanas
Archipelago
Manaus
Rio Solimões
Rio Purus
Rio Madeira
Rio Juruá
AMAZÔNIA
BR 317
Porto Velho
ACRE
Rio Branco
BR 364
RONDÔNIA
PERU
Cuzco
BOLIVIA
La Paz
Sucre
PACIFIC
OCEAN
PARAGUAY
CHILE
CORDILLERA DE ANDES
Asunción
Valparaíso
Santiago
ARGENTINA

FRENCH GUYANA
ATLANTIC OCEAN
AMAPÁ
Ilha de Marajó
Macapá
Souré
Belém
Rio Amazonas
Rio Pará
Santarém
BR 230
Rio Tocantins
BR 010
São Luís
BR 222
Fortaleza
RIO GRANDE DO NORTE
Teresina
PARÁ
MARANHÃO
Rio Tapajós
Maranhão
Rio Paranaíba
PIAUÍ
CEARÁ
BR 304
Natal
PARAÍBA
Campine Grande
Olinda
Recife
PERNAMBUCO
BR 153
BR 163
Rio Araguaia
TOCANTINS
ALAGÔAS
Maceió
BR 407
BAHIA
BR 101
SERGIPE
MATO GROSSO
Rio Paraguaçu
Cuiabá
BR 242
Cachoeira
Praia do Forte
Salvador
Serra Geral de Goiás
Rio São Francisco
Serra do Pinhaço
Mucugê
Chapada dos Guimarães
Cuiabá
BR 070
Brasília
BR 101
Pantanal Wetlands
Porto Seguro
Trancoso
GOIÁS
BR 040
MINAS GERAIS
Corumbá
BR 163
BR 330
MATO GROSSO DO SUL
BR 116
ESPÍRITO SANTO
BR 262
Campo Grande
Belo Horizonte
Vitória
Serra do Mantiqueira
BR 381
Rio Paraná
BR 262
Rio de Janeiro
SÃO PAULO
Itu
BR 116
Via Dutra
Búzios
RIO DE JANEIRO
Angra dos Reis
SP 330
São Paulo
Foz do Iguaçu
BR 373
Curitiba
PARAÑA
BR 116
Blumenau
ATLANTIC OCEAN
Serra do Mar
Florianópolis/ Ilha de Santa Catarina
Rio Uruguai
BR 277
Lages
SANTA CATARINA
BR 290
Porto Alegre
RIO GRANDE DO SUL

rio de janeiro

In This Chapter

Updated by Ana Lúcia do Vale

introducing rio de janeiro

RIO WAS NAMED—OR MISNAMED—BY the crew of a Portuguese ship that arrived in what is now the city on January 1, 1502. Thinking they had found the mouth of a river, instead of the bay that became known as the Baía de Guanabara (Guanabara Bay), they dubbed the spot Rio de Janeiro (January River). Sixty-five years later, on the feast of St. Sebastian, the city was founded with the official name of São Sebastião do Rio de Janeiro.

In 1736, Brazil's colonial capital was moved to Rio from Salvador and, in 1889 when the country became independent, Rio was declared the capital of the Republic of Brazil. It held this title until 1960 when the federal government was moved to Brasília.

Today, this pulsating city is synonymous with the girl from Ipanema, the dramatic Pão de Açúcar Mountain, and the wild and outrageous Carnaval (Carnival) celebrations. But Rio is also a city of stunning architecture, good museums, and marvelous food; it's a teeming metropolis where the very rich and the very poor live in uneasy proximity and where enthusiasm is boundless—and contagious.

As you leave the airport and head to your hotel, you'll be tossed onto a massive, chaotic, not-so-scenic urban roadway. But, by the time you reach breezy, sunny Avenida Atlântica—flanked on one side by white beach and azure sea and on the other by the pleasure-palace hotels that testify to the city's eternal lure—your heart will leap with expectation. Now you're truly in Rio, where the 10 million wicked angels and shimmering devils known as *cariocas* dwell.

The term "carioca" comes from the country's early history, when it meant "white man's house" and was used to describe a Portuguese trading station. Today the word defines more than birthplace, race, or residence: it represents an ethos of pride, a sensuality, and a passion for life. Much of the carioca verve comes from the sheer physical splendor of a city blessed with seemingly endless beaches and sculpted promontories.

Prepare to have your senses engaged and your inhibitions untied. You'll be seduced by a host of images: the joyous bustle of vendors at Sunday's Feira Hippie (Hippie Fair); the tipsy babble at sidewalk cafés as patrons sip their last glass of icy beer under the stars; the blanket of lights beneath Pão de Açúcar; the bikers, joggers, strollers, and power walkers who parade along the beach each morning. Borrow the carioca spirit for your stay; you may find yourself reluctant to give it back.

PORTRAITS

FÊTES AND FEASTS

If anyone knows how to party half-naked for five nights straight, cariocas do. The greatest show on earth, Carnaval, happens every year and is a sight to behold for tourists and cariocas alike. But Rio's ethnic diversity has also created a fascinating religious and artistic tradition, in which faiths and beats from Africa, Europe, and native Brazil combine in beautiful ritual, as in the seasonal rites of the Macumba faith.

Carnaval

Of the great carnivals of the world—Venice in Europe, Trinidad and Tobago in the Caribbean, and Mardi Gras in New Orleans—

Brazil's Carnaval may be the most amazing. In some areas, events begin right after Reveillon (New Year's) and continue beyond the four main days of celebration (just before the start of Lent) with smaller feasts and festivities. At Carnaval's peak, businesses close throughout the country as Brazilians don costumes—from the elaborate to the barely there—and take to the streets singing and dancing. These four explosive days of color see formal parades as well as spontaneous street parties fueled by flatbed trucks that carry bands from neighborhood to neighborhood.

While Carnaval celebrations unfold all over Brazil, there's none more glittery, glitzy, or downright decadent than Rio's. The *cariocas* (citizens of Rio) unleash a passion that sweeps across the city in over-the-top parades, pulsating street parties, and galas—all with the frenetic samba beat sizzling in the background. The highlight is the judging of the city's *escolas de samba* (samba schools, which are actually neighborhood groups, not schools at all) in two nights of glittering parades. These competitions draw some of Rio's best percussionists, dozens of lavish floats, and thousands of marchers, including statesmen, beauty queens, veteran samba musicians, soccer personalities, and would-be celebrities (even a few seconds of TV exposure marching with a samba school is enough to launch a modeling or acting career). They all weave through the aptly named Sambódromo from sunset to dawn. The floats have themes that run the gamut from political to playful; in past years they've included dark commentaries on the country's poor and silly tributes to plastic surgery.

Rites on the Beach

Although Rio's annual Carnaval is an amazing spectacle, there is perhaps no stranger sight than that which takes place on the beaches each New Year's Eve. Under the warm tropical sky and with the backdrop of the modern city, thousands faithful to the Macumba religion honor Iemanjá, the goddess of the sea.

The advent of the new year is a time for renewal and to ask for blessings. The faithful—of all ages, colors, and classes—determined to start the year right, pour onto the beaches at around 10 PM. Some draw mystic signs in the sand. Others lay out white tablecloths with gifts befitting a proud, beautiful goddess: combs, mirrors, lipsticks, hair ribbons, perfumes, wines. Still others bring flowers with notes asking for favors tucked amid the blossoms. Worshipers chant and sing over their offerings and set candles around them.

By 11:30 PM, the beaches are a mass of white-clad believers with flickering candles—the shore looks as if it has been invaded by millions of fireflies. At midnight, the singing, shrieking, and sobbing is accompanied by fireworks, sirens, and bells. The faithful rush to the water for the moment of truth: if the goddess is satisfied with an offering, it's carried out to sea, and the gift giver's wish will come true. If, however, Iemanjá is displeased with an offering, the ocean will throw it back; the gift giver must try again another year.

BLAME IT ON THE BOSSA NOVA—OR THE SAMBA, OR THE FORRÓ, OR THE MAXIXE . . .

Nothing in the world sounds like the music of Brazil. Whether you're listening to a rousing samba on a restaurant radio, a soothing bossa nova in a beachside café, or an uplifting Afro-Brazilian spiritist song on the street, you know instantly that you're hearing the country's beating heart. And even a short list of musical styles—which are as often linked to rhythms and dances as they are to tunes and lyrics—rolls off the tongue like an ancient chant: *axé, bossa nova, forró, frevo, samba, tropicalismo.* Many of these are divided into subcategories, with varying types of lyrics, singing styles, arrangements, and instrumentation. Some also fall into the supercategory of *música popular brasileira* (MPB; Brazilian popular music). All fill the ear with a seamless and enchanting blend of European, African, Indian, and regional Brazilian sound.

Samba, the music for which Brazil is perhaps most famous, is believed to have its roots in *lundu*, a Bantu rhythm reminiscent of a fandango yet characterized by a hip-swiveling style of dance, and *maxixe*, a mixture of polka as well as Portuguese and African rhythms. The earliest references to samba appear in the late 19th century, and one theory suggests the term comes from the Bantu word *semba*, meaning "gyrating movement." "Pelo Telefone" ("On the Telephone"), the first song actually designated as a samba, was recorded in 1917. By the 1930s, the samba was being played in Rio de Janeiro's Carnaval parades, and by the 1960s it was the indisputable music of Carnaval. Today its many forms include the pure samba *de morro* (literally, "of the hill"; figuratively, "of the poor neighborhood"), which is performed using only percussion instruments, and the samba *canção* (the more familiar "samba song").

From the samba came two more MPB genres: The bossa nova (a slang term that's akin to "new way" or, even, "new wave") and tropicalismo. Bossa nova—a blend of mellow samba, cool American jazz, and French impressionism—began in the late 1950s in Rio's chic Zona Sul neighborhoods of Copacabana, Ipanema, and Leblon. Its innovators included the classically trained composer, Tom Jobim; the poet and diplomat, Vinicius de Moraes; and the northeastern guitarist, João Gilberto, and his wife and singer, Astrud Gilberto. The politically turbulent '60s and '70s saw the development of tropicalismo. Such northeastern musicians and intellectuals as Caetano Veloso, Chico Buarque, and Giberto Gil combined contemporary instruments (including the electric guitar and keyboard) and avant-garde experimentation with samba and other traditional rhythms. Often the tunes were upbeat even though the lyrics were highly critical of social injustice and political tyranny. The tropicalismo movement, though popular with the people, was frowned upon by the military regime. Some of its performers were arrested; others, including Veloso and Buarque, had to live abroad for several years.

Of late, Jamaican reggae has been added to the Brazilian mix. Gilberto Gil's recordings of classic Bob Marley songs, including "No Woman, No Cry," honor their source and yet have a richness all their own. The dreadlocked singer Carlinhos Brown and his group, Timbalada, blend reggae sounds with the traditional rhythms of northeastern Brazil.

— *by Alan Ryan*

THE BEAUTIFUL GAME

Brazilians are mad about *futebol* (soccer), their "jogo bonito," and players here are fast and skillful. The best possess *jinga*, a quality that translates roughly as feline, almost swaggering grace. Some of their ball-handling moves are so fluid they seem more akin to ballet—or at least to the samba—than to sport.

Futebol is believed to have been introduced in the late 19th century by employees of British-owned firms. By the early 20th century, upper-class Brazilians had formed their own leagues, as had the nation's European immigrants, who were already familiar with the game. Because it requires little equipment, the sport also found a following in Brazil's poor communities.

You can see young *brasileiros* everywhere practicing—any of these boys could be a future futebol hero. Brazil has turned out many international stars: the most famous, Pelé, retired more than 20 years ago and is still revered as a national hero. The country's team is consistently included in World Cup competitions and is a repeat title holder.

Fans come to games with musical instruments, flags, banners, streamers, talcum powder, and firecrackers. There's no better spot for the brave to witness the spectacle than at the world's largest soccer stadium, Rio's Estádio Maracanã. Here, you and 219,999 other people can make merry. Even if you don't have a great view of the field, you'll certainly be a part of the event.

QUICK TOURS

If you're here for just a short period you need to plan carefully so you don't miss the must-see sights. The following itineraries will help you structure your visit efficiently. See Here and There for more information about individual sights.

TOUR ONE

You must visit Rio's two most famous peaks: take the cable car to Pão de Açúcar in the morning and visit Corcovado—and the nearby Museu de Arte Naif do Brasil—that afternoon. If your tour falls on a weekday, swing by the little Museu Carmen Miranda to see the Brazilian bombshell's costumes, jewelry, and wild headdresses. In the evening, join the fun at a samba show at Plataforma.

TOUR TWO

Wander through historic Centro. Have lunch at the opulent Café do Teatro, and hop the metrô to the Palácio do Catete. Then take the Santa Teresa trolley to the Museu Chácara do Céu.

TOUR THREE

No matter how short your stay in Rio, the sun and sand will be irresistible. Stroll from Copacabana to Ipanema, stopping en route to order a tropical pizza at Bar Garota de Ipanema, or grab an icy drink and settle in under a beach umbrella. If your tour falls on a Sunday, do some souvenir shopping at Ipanema's Feira Hippie. Wind up the day by trying Brazil's national dish at Casa da Feijoada.

In This Chapter

Updated by Ana Lúcia do Vale

here and there

CARIOCAS DIVIDE THEIR CITY into three sections: Zona Norte (North Zone), Zona Sul (South Zone), and Centro, the downtown area that separates them. Except for some museums, churches, and historic sights, most of the tourist activity is in beach- and hotel-laden Zona Sul. To sense the carioca spirit, spend a day on Copacabana and walk from the Avenida Atlântica to Ipanema. The western extension of Ipanema, Leblon, is an affluent, intimate community flush with good, small restaurants and bars (sadly, the water is polluted). The more distant southern beaches, beginning with São Conrado and extending past Barra da Tijuca to Grumari, become richer in natural beauty and increasingly isolated.

Although Rio's settlement dates back nearly 500 years, it's in every respect a modern city. Most of the historic structures have fallen victim to the wrecking ball, though a few churches and villas are still tucked in and around Centro. As these colonial vestiges are far-flung, consider seeing them on an organized walking or bus tour. You can use the metrô (and comfortable walking shoes) to explore, or the bus is another option. Just be sure you know where you're going, and memorize some key phrases in Portuguese as bus drivers don't speak English. Police have put a dent in crime, but as in any large city, be cautious and aware.

CENTRO AND ENVIRONS

What locals generally refer to as Centro is a sprawling collection of several districts that contain the city's oldest neighborhoods, churches, and most enchanting cafés. Rio's beaches, broad boulevards, and modern architecture may be impressive; but its colonial structures, old narrow streets, and alleyways in leafy inland neighborhoods are no less so.

Numbers in the text correspond to numbers in the margin and on the Rio Centro and Environs map.

A Good Tour (or Two)

Start at the **MOSTEIRO DE SÃO BENTO** ① for your first taste of Brazilian baroque architecture. From here, move south into the heart of Centro. At the beginning of Avenida Presidente Vargas you'll find the solid **IGREJA DE NOSSA SENHORA DA CANDELÁRIA** ②. From this church there are several options: soccer fans can take a cab or the metrô to **MARACANÃ** soccer stadium, where *o jogo bonito* (the beautiful game) is played; those who prefer a more bucolic setting can head (by cab or metrô) to **QUINTA DA BOA VISTA**; and history buffs can walk south along Avenida 1° de Março, crossing it and heading west to a network of narrow lanes and alleys highlighted by the **BECO DO COMÉRCIO** ③, a pedestrian street. After wandering this area, return to Avenida 1° de Março and walk southeast to the Praça 15 de Novembro, a square that's dominated by the **PAÇO IMPERIAL** ④. A few blocks away is the large **MUSEU HISTÓRICO NACIONAL** ⑤.

From the Museu Histórico Nacional, follow Rua Santa Luzia southeast to Avenida Rio Branco, Centro's main thoroughfare. North one block is the Victorian **BIBLIOTECA NACIONAL** ⑥, and one block up from it is the French neoclassical **MUSEU NACIONAL DE BELAS ARTES** ⑦. In the middle of the next block up, and across Rio Branco, you'll find the **TEATRO**

MUNICIPAL ⑧ and its elegant café. Continue north on Rio Branco and turn left on Avenida Almirante Barroso. A short walk northwest brings you to the Largo da Carioca, a large square near the Carioca metrô stop. Atop a low hill overlooking it are the **IGREJA DE SÃO FRANCISCO DA PENITÊNCIA** ⑨ and the **CONVENTO DO SANTO ANTÔNIO** ⑩. The architecturally striking (or absurd, depending on your viewpoint) **CATEDRAL DE SÃO SEBASTIÃO DO RIO DE JANEIRO** ⑪ is just south, off Avenida República do Chile, as is the station where you can take a *bonde* (trolley) over the **AQUEDUTO DA CARIOCA** ⑫ and along charming Rua Joaquim Murtinho into Santa Teresa. This eccentric neighborhood is famed for its cobblestone streets and its popular **MUSEU CHÁCARA DO CÉU** ⑬, whose works are displayed in a magnificent former home with beautiful city views.

TIMING AND PRECAUTIONS

Although you can follow this tour in a day if you set out early, you might want to break it up into two days or be selective about which museums you fully explore. You can also mix some of the southernmost sights in with those (the Aterro do Flamengo, Museu de Arte Moderna, or Monumento aos Pracinhas) in the Flamengo, Botafogo, and Pão de Açúcar tours. However you organize your day, you'll need plenty of energy to get everything in. Leave your camera at your hotel if you're planning to use public transportation. Wear no jewelry, and keep your cash in a money belt or safe pocket.

Sights to See

⓬ **AQUEDUTO DA CARIOCA.** The imposing Carioca Aqueduct, with its 42 massive stone arches, was built between 1744 and 1750 to carry water from the Rio Carioca in the hillside neighborhood of Santa Teresa to Centro. In 1896 the city transportation company converted the then-abandoned aqueduct to a viaduct, laying trolley tracks along it. Since then, Rio's distinctive trolley cars (called "bondes" because they were financed by foreign bonds)

rio centro and environs

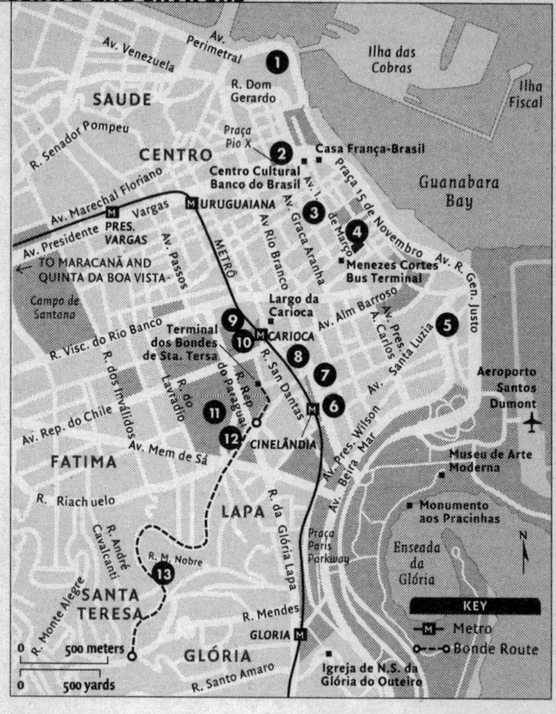

Aqueduto da Carioca, 12

Beco do Comércio, 3

Biblioteca Nacional, 6

Catedral de São Sebastião do Rio de Janeiro, 11

Convento do Santo Antônio, 10

Igreja de Nossa Senhora da Candelária, 2

Igreja de São Francisco da Penitência, 9

Mosteiro de São Bento, 1

Museu Chácara do Céu, 13

Museu Histórico Nacional, 5

Museu Nacional de Belas Artes, 7

Paço Imperial, 4

Teatro Municipal, 8

have carried people between Santa Teresa and Centro. (Guard your belongings particularly closely when you ride the open-sided bondes; the fare is about R$1.) *Metrô: Carioca or Cinelândia.*

3 **BECO DO COMÉRCIO.** A network of narrow streets and alleys centers on this pedestrian thoroughfare. The area is flanked by restored 18th-century homes, now converted to offices. The best known is the Edifício Telles de Menezes. A famous arch, the Arco dos Telles, links this area with Praça 15 de Novembro. *Praça 15 de Novembro 34, Centro. Metrô: Uruguaiana.*

6 **BIBLIOTECA NACIONAL.** Corinthian columns adorn the neoclassical National Library (built between 1905 and 1908), the first such establishment in Latin America. Its original archives were brought to Brazil by King João VI in 1808. Today it contains roughly 13 million books, including two 15th-century printed Bibles, and manuscript New Testaments from the 11th and 12th centuries; first-edition Mozart scores as well as scores by Carlos Gomes (who adapted the José de Alencar novel about Brazil's Indians, *O Guarani*, into an opera of the same name); books that belonged to Empress Teresa Christina; and many other manuscripts, prints, and drawings. Tours aren't available in English, but the devoted staff of docents will try to work something out to accommodate English-speaking book lovers. *Av. Rio Branco 219, tel. 021/2262–8255. Tours R$2. Weekdays 9–8, Sat. 9–3; tours: weekdays at 11, 1, 3, and 5. Metrô: Cinelândia.*

11 **CATEDRAL DE SÃO SEBASTIÃO DO RIO DE JANEIRO.** The exterior of this metropolitan cathedral (circa 1960), which looks like a concrete beehive, can be off-putting (as the daring modern design stands in sharp contrast to the baroque style of other churches). But don't judge untilyou've stepped inside. Outstanding stained-glass windows transform the interior—which is 80 m (263 ft) high and 96 m (315 ft) in diameter—into a warm yet serious place of worship that accommodates up to 20,000 people. An 8½-ton granite rock lends considerable weight to the concept of an altar. *Av. República do Chile 245, tel. 021/2240–2869. Free. Daily 7–5:30. Metrô: Carioca or Cinelândia.*

10 **CONVENTO DO SANTO ANTÔNIO.** The Convent of St. Anthony was completed in 1780, but some parts date from 1615, making it one of Rio's oldest structures. Its baroque interior contains priceless colonial art—including wood carvings and wall paintings. The sacristy is covered with *azulejos* (Portuguese tiles). Note that the church has no bell tower: its bells hang from a double arch on the monastery ceiling. An exterior mausoleum contains the tombs of the offspring of Dom Pedro I and Dom Pedro II. *Largo da Carioca 5, tel. 021/2262–0129. Free. Weekdays 2–5. Metrô: Carioca.*

2 **IGREJA DE NOSSA SENHORA DA CANDELÁRIA.** The classic symmetry of Candelária's white dome and bell towers casts an unexpected air of sanity over the chaos of downtown traffic. The church was built on the site of a chapel founded in 1610 by Antônio de Palma after he survived a shipwreck; paintings in the present dome tell his tale. Construction on the present church began in 1775, and although it was formally dedicated by the emperor in 1811, work on the dome wasn't completed until 1877. The sculpted bronze doors were exhibited at the 1889 world's fair in Paris. *Praça Pio X, tel. 021/2233–2324. Free. Weekdays 7:30–noon and 1–4:30, weekends 8–1. Metrô: Uruguaiana.*

9 **IGREJA DE SÃO FRANCISCO DA PENITÊNCIA.** The church was completed in 1737, nearly four decades after it was started. Today it's famed for its wooden sculptures and rich gold-leaf interior. The nave contains a painting of St. Francis, the patron of the church—reportedly the first painting in Brazil done in perspective. *Largo da Carioca 5, tel. 021/2262–0197. By appointment. Metrô: Carioca.*

OFF THE BEATEN PATH **MARACANÃ** – From the Igreja de Nossa Senhora da Candelária, you can walk 3½ blocks to the Uruguaiana station and take the metrô to the world's largest soccer stadium. Officially called Estádio Mario Filho after a famous journalist, it's best known as Maracanã, for the neighborhood in which it's situated and for a nearby river. The 178,000-seat stadium (with standing room for another 42,000) went up in record time to host the 1950 World Cup. Brazil lost its chance at the cup by losing a match 2–1 to Uruguay—a game that's still analyzed a half century later. Here soccer star Pelé made his 1,000th goal in 1969. The smaller, 17,000-seat arena in the same complex has hosted events featuring such notables as Madonna, Paul McCartney, and Pope John Paul II. Stadium tours are offered daily (except on match days) from 9 to 5. *Rua Prof. Eurico Rabelo, Gate 16, tel. 021/2568–9962. R$3. Metrô: Maracanã.*

---

11 **MOSTEIRO DE SÃO BENTO.** Just a glimpse of this church's main altar will fill you with awe. Layer upon layer of curvaceous wood carvings—coated in gold—create a sense of movement. Spiral columns whirl upward to capitals topped by cherubs so chubby and angels so purposeful they seem almost animated. Although the Benedictines arrived in 1586, they didn't begin work on this church and monastery until 1617. It was completed in 1641, but such artisans as Mestre Valentim (who designed the silver chandeliers) continued to add details almost through to the 19th century. On some Sundays, mass is accompanied by Gregorian chants. *Rua Dom Gerardo 32, tel. 021/2291–7122. Free. Weekdays 8–11 and 2:30–5:30.*

★ 13 **MUSEU CHÁCARA DO CÉU.** With its cobblestone streets and bohemian atmosphere, Santa Teresa is a delightfully eccentric neighborhood. Gabled Victorian mansions sit beside alpine-style chalets as well as more prosaic dwellings—many hanging at unbelievable angles from the flower-encrusted hills. Set here, too, is the quaintly named Museum of the Small Farm of the Sky. The outstanding collection of mostly modern works was left—along with the hilltop house that contains it—by one of Rio's greatest arts patrons, Raymundo de Castro Maya. Included are originals by such 20th-century masters as Pablo Picasso, Georges Braque, Salvador Dalí, Edgar Degas, Henri Matisse, Amedeo Modigliani, and Claude Monet. The Brazilian holdings include priceless 17th- and 18th-century maps and works by leading modernists. The grounds afford fine views of the aqueduct, Centro, and the bay. *Rua Murtinho Nobre 93, tel. 021/2507–1932. Free. Wed.–Mon. noon–5.*

NEED A BREAK? Santa Teresa attracts artists, musicians, and intellectuals to its eclectic slopes. Their hangout is **BAR DO ARNAUDO** (Rua Almirante Alexandrino 316-B, tel. 021/2252–7246), which is always full.

---

5 **MUSEU HISTÓRICO NACIONAL.** The building that houses the National History Museum dates from 1762, though some sections—such as the battlements—were erected as early as 1603. It seems appropriate that this colonial structure should exhibit relics that document Brazil's history. Among its treasures are rare papers, Latin American coins, carriages, cannons, and religious art. *Praça Marechal Ancora, tel. 021/2550–9266. Free. Tues.–Fri. 10–5:30, weekends 2–6. Metrô: Carioca or Cinelândia.*

7 **MUSEU NACIONAL DE BELAS ARTES.** Works by Brazil's leading 19th- and 20th-century artists fill the space at the National Museum of Fine Arts. Although the most notable canvases are those by the country's best-known modernist, Cândido Portinari, be on the lookout for such gems as Leandro Joaquim's heartwarming 18th-century painting of Rio (at once primitive and classical, the small oval canvas seems a window on a time when fishermen still cast nets in the waters below the landmark Igreja de Nossa Senhora da Glória do Outeiro). After wandering the picture galleries, consider touring the extensive collections of folk and African art. *Av. Rio Branco 199, tel. 021/2240–0068. R$8, free Sun. Tues.–Fri. 10–6, weekends 2–6. Metrô: Carioca or Cinelândia.*

4 **PAÇO IMPERIAL.** This two-story colonial building is notable for its thick stone walls and ornate entrance. It was built in 1743, and for the next 60 years was the headquarters for Brazil's captains (viceroys), appointed by the Portuguese court in Lisbon. When King João VI arrived, he made it his royal palace. After Brazil's

declaration of independence, emperors Dom Pedro I and II called the palace home. When the monarchy was overthrown, the building became Rio's central post office. Restoration work in the 1980s transformed it into a cultural center and concert hall. The third floor has a restaurant, and a ground-floor shop sells stationery and CDs. The square on which the palace is set, Praça 15 de Novembro, has witnessed some of Brazil's most significant historic moments. Known in colonial days as Largo do Paço, here two emperors were crowned, slavery was abolished, and Emperor Pedro II was deposed. Its modern name is a reference to the date of the declaration of the Republic of Brazil: November 15, 1889. *Praça 15 de Novembro 48, Centro, tel. 021/2533–4407. Free. Tues.–Sun. noon–6:30.*

OFF THE BEATEN PATH **QUINTA DA BOA VISTA** – West of downtown, set in the entrancing landscaped grounds of a former royal estate, you'll find pools and marble statues as well as the Museu Nacional and the Jardim Zoológico. Housed in what was once the imperial palace (circa 1803), the museum has exhibits on Brazil's past and on its flora, fauna, and minerals—including the biggest meteorite (5 tons) found in the southern hemisphere. At the zoo, you can see animals from Brazil's wilds in re-creations of their natural habitats. A highlight is the Nocturnal House, where you can spot such night creatures as bats and sloths. *Entrance at corner of Av. Paulo e Silva and Av. Bartolomeu de Gusmão, tel. 021/2568–8262 for museum; 021/2569–2024 for zoo. R$3 for museum; R$4 for zoo. Tues.–Sun. 9–4:30. Metrô: San Cristóvão.*

---

8 **TEATRO MUNICIPAL.** Carrara marble, stunning mosaics, glittering chandeliers, bronze and onyx statues, gilded mirrors, German stained-glass windows, brazilwood inlay floors, and murals by Brazilian artists Eliseu Visconti and Rodolfo Amoedo make the Municipal Theater opulent, indeed. Opened in 1909, it's a scaled-down version of the Paris Opera House. The main entrance and first two galleries are particularly ornate. As you climb to the

upper floors, the decor becomes more ascetic, a reflection of a time when different classes entered through different doors and sat in separate sections. The theater seats 2,357—with outstanding sight lines—for its dance performances and classical music concerts. Tours are available by appointment. *Praça Floriano 210, tel. 021/2297–4411. Metrô: Cinelândia or Carioca.*

NEED A BREAK? Elegance joins good food at the charming **CAFÉ DO TEATRO** (Praça Floriano 210, tel. 021/2297–4411), in the lower level of the Teatro Municipal. Have a light lunch (weekdays 11–3) or coffee and a pastry (served at lunch or during evening performances) as you drink in the atmosphere. The decor is classical, replete with columns and wall mosaics that look like something out of a Cecil B. DeMille epic. The bar resembles a sarcophagus, and two sphinxes flank the sunken dining area. Note that this is one of the few cafés where you may be turned away if you're dressed too shabbily.

FLAMENGO, BOTAFOGO, AND PÃO DE AÇÚCAR

These neighborhoods and their most famous peak—Pão de Açúcar—are like a bridge between the southern beach districts and Centro. Several highways intersect here, making it a hub for drives to Corcovado, Copacabana, Barra, or Centro. The metrô also travels through the area. Although the districts are largely residential, you'll find Rio Sul, one of the city's most popular shopping centers, as well as good museums and fabulous public spaces.

The eponymous beach at Flamengo no longer draws swimmers (its gentle waters look appealing but are polluted; the people you see are sunning, not swimming). A marina sits on a bay at one end of the beach, which is connected via a busy boulevard to the smaller beach (also polluted), at Botafogo. This neighborhood is home to the city's yacht club, and when Rio was Brazil's capital, it was also the site of the city's glittering embassy row. The embassies were long ago transferred to Brasília, but the mansions that housed them remain. Among Botafogo's more interesting mansion- and tree-lined streets are Mariana, Sorocaba, Matriz, and Visconde e Silva.

Botafogo faces tiny sheltered Urca, which is separated by Pão de Açúcar from a small patch of yellow sand called Vermelha. This beach is, in turn, blocked by the Urubu and Leme mountains from the 1-km (½-mi) Leme Beach at the start of the Zona Sul.

Numbers in the text correspond to numbers in the margin and on the Rio de Janeiro City map.

A Good Tour

Start at the northern end of the lovely, landscaped **ATERRO DO FLAMENGO** and the **MUSEU DE ARTE MODERNA (MAM)** ⑭. Nearby is the **MONUMENTO AOS PRACINHAS** ⑮, which honors the dead of World War II. Wander south along the Aterro before hopping into a cab and heading inland to the hilltop **IGREJA DE NOSSA SENHORA DA GLÓRIA DO OUTEIRO** ⑯. Get on the metrô at the Glória station and take it one stop to the Catete terminal, or walk south along Rua da Glória da Lapa to Rua da Catete, and you'll find the **PALÁCIO DO CATETE** ⑰. From here you can either return to the Aterro by cab and walk south to the **MUSEU CARMEN MIRANDA** ⑱, or you can take the metrô to the Botafogo stop and the nearby **CASA RUI BARBOSA** ⑲. Finish the tour by riding the cable car up the **PÃO DE AÇÚCAR** ⑳ for panoramic views of the bay and the neighborhoods you've just explored.

TIMING AND PRECAUTIONS

This tour takes a full day and involves a lot of walking and time outdoors. You can shorten the itinerary by taking a cab to sights off the Aterro do Flamengo and/or from one end of the Aterro to the other. As always, keep your money and other valuables out of sight while strolling.

Sights to See

ATERRO DO FLAMENGO. This waterfront park flanks Baía de Guanabara from the Glória neighborhood to Flamengo. It gets its name from its location atop an *aterro* (landfill), and was designed by landscape architect Roberto Burle Marx. Paths used for jogging, walking, and biking wind through it. There are also playgrounds and public tennis and basketball courts. On weekends the freeway beside the park is closed to traffic; the entire area becomes one enormous public space.

19 **CASA RUI BARBOSA.** Slightly inland from the Aterro is a museum in what was once the house of 19th-century Brazilian statesmen and scholar Rui Barbosa (a liberal from Bahia State who drafted one of Brazil's early constitutions). The pink mansion dates from 1849 and contains memorabilia of Barbosa's life, including his 1913 car and an extensive library that's often consulted by scholars from around the world. During the ongoing reconstruction, admission is free. *Rua São Clemente 134, Botafogo, tel. 021/2537–0036. Free. Tues.–Fri. 9–4, weekends 2–5. Metrô: Botafogo.*

16 **IGREJA DE NOSSA SENHORA DA GLÓRIA DO OUTEIRO.** Set atop a hill, this baroque church is visible from many spots in the city, making it a landmark that's truly cherished by the cariocas. Its location was a strategic point in the city's early days. Estácio da Sá took this hill from the French in the 1560s and then went on to expand the first settlement and found a city for the Portuguese. The church, which wasn't built until 1739, is notable for its octagonal floor plan, large dome, ornamental stonework, and vivid tilework. *Praça Nossa Senhora da Glória 135, Glória, tel. 021/2557–4600. Free. Tues.–Fri. 9–noon and 1–5, weekends 9–noon. Tours first Sun. of month by appt. only. Metrô: Glória.*

15 **MONUMENTO AOS PRACINHAS.** The Monument to the Brazilian Dead of World War II (the nation sided with the Allies during the conflict) is actually a museum and monument combined. It houses military uniforms, medals, stamps, and documents belonging to soldiers. Two soaring columns flank the tomb of an

unknown soldier. The first Sunday of each month, Brazil's armed forces perform a colorful changing of the guard. *Parque Brigadeiro Eduardo Gomes, Flamengo, tel. 021/2240–1283. Free. Tues.–Sun. 10–4. Metrô: Cinelândia.*

14 **MUSEU DE ARTE MODERNA (MAM).** Set in a striking concrete-and-glass building, the Modern Art Museum has a collection of some 1,700 works by artists from Brazil and elsewhere. It also hosts significant special exhibitions, and has a movie theater that plays art films. *Av. Infante Dom Henrique 85, Flamengo, tel. 021/2210–2188. Free. Tues.–Sun. noon–6. Metrô: Cinelândia.*

18 **MUSEU CARMEN MIRANDA.** This tribute to the Brazilian bombshell is in a circular building that resembles a concrete spaceship (its door even opens up rather than out). On display are some of the elaborate costumes and incredibly high platform shoes worn by the actress, who was viewed as a national icon by some and as a traitor to true Brazilian culture by others. Hollywood photos of Miranda, who was only 46 when she died of a heart attack in 1955, show her in her trademark turban and jewelry. You'll also find her records, movie posters, and such memorabilia as the silver hand-held mirror she was clutching when she died. *Av. Rui Barbosa 560, Flamengo, tel. 021/2551–2597. Free. Weekdays 11–5. Metrô: Flamengo.*

NEED A BREAK? Flamengo contains some of Rio's better small restaurants. For authentic Brazilian fare, the bohemian community heads to **LAMAS** (Rua Marques de Abrantes 18, tel. 021/2556–0799).

★ 17 **PALÁCIO DO CATETE.** Once the villa of a German baron, the elegant, 19th-century, granite-and-marble palace became the presidential residence after the 1889 coup overthrew the monarchy and established the Republic of Brazil. Eighteen presidents lived here.

You can gaze at the palace's gleaming parquet floors and intricate bas-relief ceilings as you wander through its **Museu da**

rio de janeiro city

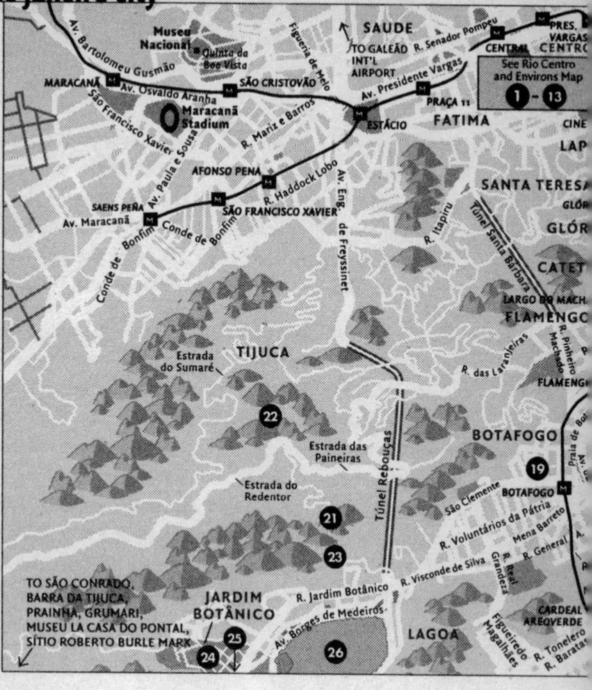

Casa Rui Barbosa, **19**

Corcovado, **21**

Floresta da Tijuca, **22**

Igreja de Nossa Senhora da Glória do Outeiro, **16**

Jardim Botânico, **24**

Jóquei Clube, **25**

Lagoa Rodrigo de Freitas, **26**

Monumento aos Pracinhas, **15**

Museu de Arte Moderna (MAM), **14**

Museu de Arte Naif do Brasil, **23**

Museu Carmen Miranda, **18**

Palácio do Catete, **17**

Pão d'Açúcar, **20**

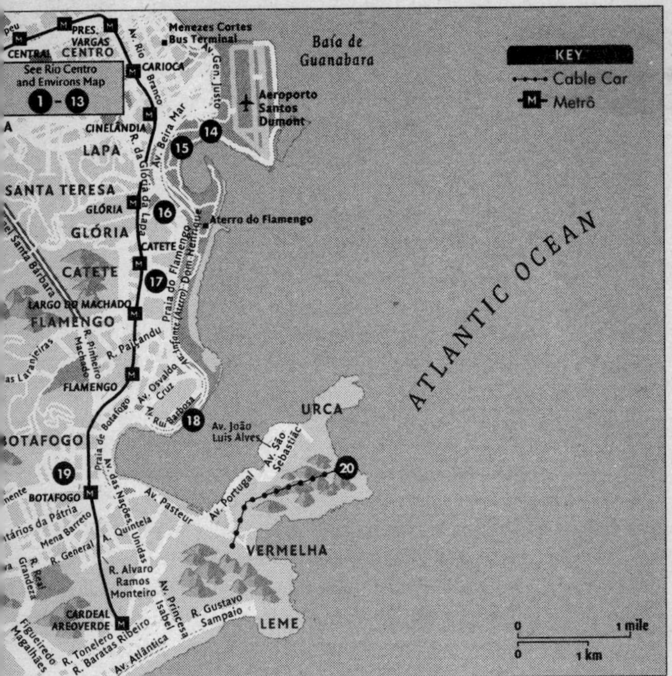

PRES. VARGAS
CENTRAL
CENTRO
See Rio Centro and Environs Map 1 - 13
CARIOCA
CINELÂNDIA
LAPA
SANTA TERESA
GLÓRIA
GLÓRIA
CATETE
CATETE
LARGO DO MACHADO
FLAMENGO
FLAMENGO
BOTAFOGO
BOTAFOGO
CARDEAL AREOVERDE
URCA
VERMELHA
LEME
Menezes Cortes Bus Terminal
Baía de Guanabara
Aeroporto Santos Dumont
Aterro do Flamengo
ATLANTIC OCEAN
Av. Rio Branco
Av. Gen. Justo
Av. Beira Mar
R. da Glória da Lapa
Praia do Flamengo
Av. Infante (Aterro) Dom Henrique
R. Paiçandu
R. Pinheiro Machado
Av. Osvaldo Cruz
Av. Rui Barbosa
Av. João Luís Alves
Av. São Sebastião
Av. Portugal
Av. Pasteur
Praia de Botafogo
Av. das Nações Unidas
Mena Barreto
R. General
A. Quintela
R. Alvaro Ramos Monteiro
R. Real Grandeza
Av. Princesa Isabel
R. Gustavo Sampaio
R. Tonelero
R. Baratas Ribeiro
Av. Atlântica
Figueiredo Magalhães
KEY
Cable Car
Metrô
0 1 mile
0 1 km

República (Museum of the Republic). The permanent—and frank—exhibits include a shroud-draped view of the bedroom where President Getúlio Vargas committed suicide in 1954 after the military threatened to overthrow his government. Presidential memorabilia, furniture, and paintings that date from the proclamation of the republic to the end of Brazil's military regime in 1985 are also displayed. A small contemporary art gallery and a theater operate within the museum. *Rua do Catete 153, Catete, tel. 021/2558–6350. R$5, free Wed. Tues.–Sun. noon–5, weekends 2–6. Metrô: Catete.*

★ 20 **PÃO DE AÇÚCAR.** This soaring 1,300-m (390-ft) granite block at the mouth of Baía de Guanabara was originally called *pau-nh-acugua* (high, pointed peak) by the indigenous Tupi Indians. To the Portuguese the phrase seemed similar to *pão de açúcar*, or "sugarloaf"; the rock's shape reminded them of the conical loaves in which refined sugar was sold. Italian-made bubble cars holding 75 passengers each move up the mountain in two stages. The first stop is at Morro da Urca, a smaller, 212-m (705-ft) mountain; the second is at the summit of Pão de Açúcar itself. The trip to each level takes three minutes. In high season, long lines form for the cable car; the rest of the year, the wait is seldom more than 30 minutes. *Av. Pasteur 520, Praia Vermelha, Urca, tel. 021/2546–8400. R$18. Daily 8 AM–10 PM.*

ZONA SUL

Rio is home to 23 *praias* (beaches), an almost continuous 73-km (45-mi) ribbon of sand. All are public and are served by buses and taxis. At intervals along the beaches at Copacabana and Ipanema are small *postos* (bathhouses) with washrooms, showers, and dressing rooms that can be used for about R$2. Kiosks manned by police also pepper the avenues running parallel to the beach, and crime has dropped dramatically as a result.

A Good Beach Strategy

Although the circuit starts to the northeast at the beaches of Flamengo, Botafogo, Urca, and Vermelha, the waters off their shores are often polluted. The best sands are farther south. Leme, which is popular with senior citizens, runs into the city's grande dame, **COPACABANA.** Its 3-km (2-mi) stretch is lined by a sidewalk whose swirling pattern was designed by Roberto Burle Marx. You'll also find outdoor cafés, high-rise hotels, and juice kiosks. At the end, cut around on the small Arpoador Beach (favored by surfers), or take Avenida Francisco Otaviano to **IPANEMA.** Note that the final leg of this beach, called Leblon, is polluted; swimming isn't recommended.

Beyond Ipanema and Leblon, mountains again form a natural wall separating you from the next beach, little Vidigal. Still more mountains block it from **SÃO CONRADO,** a beach where hang gliders land after leaping from a nearby peak. A highway through a mountain tunnel forms the link between São Conrado and the long, spectacular **BARRA DA TIJUCA.** Its waters are clean and cool, and its far end, known as Recreio dos Bandeirantes, was home to a small fishing village until the late 1960s. Beyond are **PRAINHA,** whose rough seas make it popular with surfers, and the lovely **GRUMARI,**whose copper sands are often packed. Just before Prainha, you can take a slight detour to visit the **MUSEU CASA DO PONTAL,** Brazil's largest folk-art museum. It's worth continuing down the hill beyond Grumari to the **SÍTIO ROBERTO BURLE MARX** for an in-depth look at one of Brazil's greatest artists.

City buses and small green minivans pick you up and drop you off wherever you request along the shore. If you're brave enough to drive, the city has established small, affordable parking lots (look for attendants in green-and-yellow vests) along waterfront avenues. There are several organized tours that take in the beaches, and agents at Turismo Clássico can arrange for drivers and guides.

TIMING AND PRECAUTIONS

Although you can tour the shoreline in several hours, consider spending a full day just wandering from Copacabana to Ipanema or sunbathing on Barra da Tijuca. Remember that Rio's beaches aren't just about sunning and swimming; they're also about volleyball games, strolling, biking, and people-watching.

Don't shun the beaches because of reports of crime, but *do* take precautions. Leave jewelry, passports, and large sums of cash at your hotel; avoid wandering alone and at night; and be alert when groups of friendly youths engage you in conversation. (Sometimes they're trying to distract you while one of their cohorts snatches your belongings.) The biggest danger is the sun. From 10 to 3 the rays are merciless, making it essential to have heavy-duty sunscreen, hats, cover-ups, and plenty of liquids (you can also rent a beach umbrella from a vendor or your hotel). Hawkers stroll the beaches with beverages—take advantage of their services. Lifeguard stations are found once every kilometer.

Sights to See

★ **BARRA DA TIJUCA.** Cariocas consider the beach to be Rio's best, and the 18-km-long (11-mi-long) sweep of sand and jostling waves certainly is dramatic. Pollution isn't a problem, and in many places neither are crowds. Barra's water is also cooler and its breezes more refreshing than those at other beaches. The waves can be strong in spots; this attracts surfers, windsurfers, and jet skiers, but you should swim with caution. The beach is set slightly below a sidewalk, where cafés and restaurants beckon. Condos have also sprung up here, and the city's largest shopping centers and supermarkets have made inland Barra their home.

At the far end of Barra's beachfront avenue, Sernambetiba, is Recreio dos Bandeirantes, a 1-km (½-mi) stretch of sand anchored by a huge rock, which creates a small protected cove. Its quiet seclusion makes it popular with families. The calm, pollution-free water, with no waves or currents, is good for bathing, but don't try to swim around the rock—it's bigger than it looks.

COPACABANA. Maddening traffic, noise, packed apartment blocks, and a world-famous beach—this is Copacabana, Manhattan with bikinis. A walk along the neighborhood's classic crescent is a must. You'll see the essence of beach culture, a cradle-to-grave lifestyle that begins with toddlers accompanying their parents to the water and ends with graying seniors walking hand in hand along the sidewalk. It's here that athletic men play volleyball using only their feet and heads, not their hands. As you can tell by all the goal nets, soccer is also popular (Copacabana hosts the world beach soccer championships every January and February). You can swim here, although pollution levels and a strong undertow can sometimes be discouraging.

Copacabana's privileged live on beachfront Avenida Atlântica, famed for its wide mosaic sidewalks, hotels, and cafés. On weekends, two of the avenue's lanes are closed to traffic and are taken over by joggers, rollerbladers, cyclists, and pedestrians. Two blocks inland from and parallel to the beach is Avenida Nossa Senhora de Copacabana, the main commercial street, with shops, restaurants, and sidewalks crowded with the colorful characters that give Copacabana its flavor.

At the Pão de Açúcar end is Leme, a natural extension of Copacabana. A rock formation juts into the water here, forming a quiet cove that's less crowded than the rest of the beach. Along a sidewalk, at the side of the mountain overlooking Leme, anglers stand elbow to elbow with their lines dangling into the sea.

IPANEMA. As you stroll along this beach, you'll catch a cross section of the city's residents, each favoring a particular stretch. There's an area dominated by families; a spot near Copacabana, known as Arpoador, that tantalizes surfers; and even a strand favored by the gay community. Ipanema, nearby Leblon (off whose shores the waters are too polluted for swimming), and the blocks surrounding Lagoa Rodrigo de Freitas are part of Rio's money belt. For a close-up look at the posh apartment buildings, stroll down beachfront Avenida Vieira Souto and its extension, Avenida Delfim Moreira, or drive around the lagoon on Avenida Epitácio Pessoa. The tree-lined streets between Ipanema Beach and the lagoon are as peaceful as they are attractive. The boutiques along Rua Garcia D'Ávila make window-shopping a sophisticated endeavor. Other chic areas near the beach include Praça Nossa Senhora da Paz, which is lined with wonderful restaurants and bars; Rua Vinicius de Moraes; and Rua Farme de Amoedo.

NEED A BREAK? Have you ever wondered if there really *was* a girl from Ipanema? The song was inspired by schoolgirl Heloisa Pinheiro, who caught the fancy of songwriter Antônio Carlos (a.k.a. Tom) Jobim and his pal lyricist Vinicius de Moraes as she walked past the two bohemians sitting in their favorite bar. They then penned one of last century's classics. That was in 1962, and today the bar has been renamed **BAR GAROTA DE IPANEMA** (Rua Vinicius de Moraes 49-A, Ipanema, tel. 021/2267–8787).

OFF THE BEATEN PATH **MUSEU CASA DO PONTAL** – If you're heading toward Prainha or beyond to Grumari, consider taking a detour to Brazil's largest folk-art museum. One room houses a wonderful mechanical sculpture that represents all of the escolas de samba that march in the Carnaval parades. Another mechanical "scene" depicts a circus in action. This private collection is owned by a French expatriate, Jacques Van de Beuque, who has been collecting Brazilian treasures—including religious pieces—since he arrived in the country in 1946. *Estrada do Pontal 3295, Grumari, tel. 021/2490–3278 or 021/2539–4914. R$5. Tues.–Sun. 9–5.*

★ **PRAINHA AND GRUMARI.** The length of two football fields, Prainha is a vest-pocket beach favored by surfers, who take charge of it on weekends. Set about 35 minutes west of Ipanema on a road that hugs the coast, it's accessible only by car from Avenida Sernambetiba. The swimming is good, but watch out for surfboards. About five minutes farther, off Estrada de Guaratiba, is Grumari, a beach that seems an incarnation of paradise. What it lacks in amenities (you'll find only a couple of groupings of thatch-roof huts selling drinks and snacks) it makes up for in natural beauty: the glorious red sands of its quiet cove are backed by low, lush hills. On weekdays, especially in the off-season, these beaches are almost empty; on weekends, particularly in peak season, the road to and from them is so crowded it almost becomes a parking lot.

SÃO CONRADO. In Leblon, at the end of Ipanema blocked by the imposing Dois Irmãos Mountain, Avenida Niemeyer snakes along rugged cliffs that offer spectacular sea views on the left. The road returns to sea level again in São Conrado, a natural amphitheater surrounded by forested mountains and the ocean. Development of what is now a mostly residential area began in the late '60s with an eye on Rio's high society. A short stretch along its beach includes the condominiums of a former president, the ex-wife of another former president, an ex-governor of Rio de Janeiro State, and a one-time Central Bank president. In the middle of the small valley is the exclusive Gávea Golf and Country Club. The far end of São Conrado is marked by the towering Pedra da Gávea, a huge flat-top granite block. Next to it is Pedra Bonita, the mountain from which gliders depart. (Although this beach was the city's most popular a few years ago, contaminated water has discouraged swimmers.)

Ironically, the neighborhood is surrounded by shantytowns. Much of the high ground has been taken over by Rio's largest favela, Rocinha, where an estimated 200,000 people live. This precarious city within a city seems poised to slide down the hill.

It, and others like it, are the result of Rio's chronic housing problem coupled with the refusal by many of the city's poor to live in distant working-class neighborhoods. Though the favelas are dangerous for the uninitiated, they have their own internal order, and their tremendous expansion has even upper-class cariocas referring to them not as slums but as neighborhoods. Notice that the favelas enjoy prime vistas, and most of them are constructed of brick.

OFF THE BEATEN PATH **SÍTIO ROBERTO BURLE MARX** – Beyond Grumari the road winds through mangrove swamps and tropical forest. It's an apt setting for the plantation-turned-museum where Brazil's famous landscape designer, Roberto Burle Marx, is memorialized. Marx, the mind behind Rio's mosaic beachfront walkways and the Aterro do Flamengo, was said to have "painted with plants" and was the first designer to use Brazilian flora in his projects. More than 3,500 species—including some discovered by and named for Marx as well as many on the endangered list—flourish at this 100-acre estate. He grouped his plants not only according to their soil and light needs but also according to their shape and texture. Marx also liked to mix modern things with old ones—a recurring theme throughout the property. The results are both whimsical and elegant. In 1985 he bequeathed the farm to the Brazilian government, though he remained until his death in 1994. His house is now a cultural center full of his belongings, including collections of folk art. The grounds also contain his large, ultramodern studio (he was a painter, too) and a small, restored colonial chapel dedicated to St. Anthony. *Estrada de Guaratiba 2019, Guaratiba, tel. 021/2410–1412 or 021/2410–1171. R$4. By appointment only.*

THE LUSH INLAND

Beyond the sand and sea in the Zona Sul are lush parks and gardens as well as marvelous museums, seductive architecture, and tantalizing restaurants. You can't say you've seen Rio until you've taken in the view from Corcovado and then strolled through its forested areas or beside its inland lagoon—hanging out just like a true carioca.

Numbers in the text correspond to numbers in the margin and on the Rio de Janeiro City map.

A Good Tour

Head first to the imposing **CORCOVADO** ㉑ and its hallmark Cristo Redentor statue. As you slide up the side of the steep mountain in the train, you'll pass through the lush forested area known as **FLORESTA DA TIJUCA** ㉒. (If you want to explore the forest more, you'll need to hire a cab or join a tour that offers both Corcovado and Floresta da Tijuca.) Back down the hill and at the train station again, stroll downhill a short distance to the **MUSEU DE ARTE NAIF DO BRASIL** ㉓, which houses a renowned collection of primitive art from around the world. The same street leads uphill to the delightful colonial square called Largo do Boticário—a good place to rest your feet. From here, grab a taxi and journey west to the inviting **JARDIM BOTÂNICO** ㉔, across from which is the Jóquei Clube . The botanical gardens are within walking distance from the Lagoa Rodrigo de Freitas, the giant saltwater lagoon that serves as one of the city's playgrounds—for children and adults alike.

TIMING AND PRECAUTIONS

You can see these sights in a day if you start early. Try to visit Corcovado on a clear day, clouds often obscure the Christ statue on its summit. You can join an organized tour or hire a cabbie to take you out for the day (public transportation doesn't conveniently reach these sights). The security is good at Corcovado and Floresta da Tijuca, so you can usually carry your camera without worry. At the Jardim Botânico and the Lagoa Rodrigo de Freitas, however, be alert. Throughout this tour, keep valuables in a money belt or somewhere else out of sight.

Sights to See

★ 21 **CORCOVADO.** There's an eternal argument about which view is better, from Pão de Açúar or from here. Corcovado has two advantages: at 690 m (2,300 ft), it's nearly twice as high and offers an excellent view of Pão de Açúar itself. The sheer 300-m (1,000-ft) granite face of Corcovado (the name means "hunchback" and refers to the mountain's shape) has always been a difficult undertaking for climbers.

It wasn't until 1921, the centennial of Brazil's independence from Portugal, that someone had the idea of placing a statue atop Corcovado. A team of French artisans headed by sculptor Paul Landowski was assigned the task of erecting a statue of Christ with his arms apart as if embracing the city. (Nowadays, mischievous cariocas say Christ is getting ready to clap for his favorite escola de samba.) It took 10 years, but on October 12, 1931, the **Cristo Redentor** (Christ the Redeemer) was inaugurated. The sleek, modern figure rises more than 30 m (100 ft) from a 6-m (20-ft) pedestal and weighs 700 tons. In the evening a powerful lighting system transforms it into a dramatic icon.

There are two ways to reach the top: by cogwheel train (originally built in 1885) or by winding road through the Floresta da Tijuca. The train provides delightful views of Ipanema and Leblon (from an absurd angle of ascent) as well as a close look at the thick vegetation and the butterflies and birds it attracts. (You may wonder what those oblong medicine balls hanging from the trees are, the ones that look like spiked watermelons tied to ropes—they're *jaca*, or jackfruit.) Trains leave the **Cosme Velho station** every 30 minutes, daily 8:30–6:30, for the steep 5-km (3-mi), 17-minute ascent. Late-afternoon trains are the most popular; on weekends be prepared for a long wait. *Rua Cosme Velho 513, Cosme Velho, tel. 021/2558–1329. R$18.*

Driving up through the forest is free, but if you want to visit the statue by car, you have to pay R$5 for each person plus R$5 for parking. Whether you arrive by train, tour bus, or car, a climb up a series of steep, zigzagging staircases and landings is necessary before you get to the summit, the statue, and the viewing points. There are no elevators or ramps for wheelchairs. You'll pass little cafés and shops selling film and souvenirs along the way. Once at the top, all of Rio stretches out before you.

22 **FLORESTA DA TIJUCA.** Surrounding Corcovado is the dense, tropical Tijuca Forest. Once part of a Brazilian nobleman's estate, it's studded with exotic trees and thick jungle vines and has a delightful waterfall, the Cascatinha de Taunay. About 180 m (200 yards) beyond the waterfall is the small pink-and-purple Capela Mayrink (Mayrink Chapel), with painted panels by the 20th-century Brazilian artist Cândido Portinari.

From several points along this national park's 96 km (60 mi) of narrow, winding roads the views are breathtaking. Some of the most spectacular are from Dona Marta, on the way up Corcovado; the Emperor's Table, supposedly where Brazil's last emperor, Pedro II, took his court for picnics; and, farther down the road, the Chinese View, the area where Portuguese king João VI allegedly settled the first Chinese immigrants who came to Brazil in the early 19th century to develop tea plantations. A great way to see the forest is by Jeep; you can arrange tours through a number of agencies. *Entrance at Praça Afonso Viseu 561, Tijuca, tel. 021/2492–2253. Free. Daily 7–7.*

24 **JARDIM BOTÂNICO.** The 340-acre Botanical Garden contains more than 5,000 species of tropical and subtropical plants and trees, including 900 varieties of palms (some more than a century old) and more than 140 species of birds. The temperature is usually a good 12°C (22°F) cooler in the shady garden that was created in 1808 by Portuguese King João VI during his exile in Brazil. In 1842 the garden gained its most impressive adornment, the Avenue of the Royal Palms, 720-m-long (800-yard-long) double row of 134 soaring royal palms. Elsewhere in the gardens, the Casa dos Pilões, an old gunpowder factory, has been restored and

Smart Sightseeings

Savvy travelers and others who take their sightseeing seriously have skills worth knowing about.

DON'T PLAN YOUR VISIT IN YOUR HOTEL ROOM *Don't wait until you pull into town to decide how to spend your days. It's inevitable that there will be much more to see and do than you'll have time for: choose sights in advance.*

ORGANIZE YOUR TOURING *Note the places that most interest you on a map, and visit places that are near each other during the same morning or afternoon.*

START THE DAY WELL EQUIPPED *Leave your hotel in the morning with everything you need for the day—maps, medicines, extra film, your guidebook, rain gear, and another layer of clothing in case the weather turns cooler.*

TOUR MUSEUMS EARLY *If you're there when the doors open you'll have an intimate experience of the collection.*

EASY DOES IT *See museums in the mornings, when you're fresh, and visit sit-down attractions later on. Take breaks before you need them.*

STRIKE UP A CONVERSATION *Only curmudgeons don't respond to a smile and a polite request for information. Most people appreciate your interest in their home town. And your conversations may end up being your most vivid memories.*

GET LOST *When you do, you never know what you'll find—but you can count on it being memorable. Use your guidebook to help you get back on track. Build wandering-around time into every day.*

QUIT BEFORE YOU'RE TIRED *There's no point in seeing that one extra sight if you're too exhausted to enjoy it.*

TAKE YOUR MOTHER'S ADVICE *Go to the bathroom when you have the chance. You never know what lies ahead.*

displays objects that pertained to both the nobility and to their slaves. Also on the grounds are a library, a small café, and a gift shop that sells souvenirs with ecological themes (the shop is a product of the Earth Summit that was held in 1992). *Rua Jardim Botânico 1008, tel. 021/2294–6012. R$4. Daily 8–5.*

NEED A BREAK? Cool off with some homemade ice cream featuring a tropical twist. The flavors at **MIL FRUTAS SORVETES** (Rua J. J. Seabra, Jardim Botânico, tel. 021/2511–2550) are concocted using such local fruits as *acerola* and jaca.

★ 23 **MUSEU DE ARTE NAIF DO BRASIL.** More than 8,000 art naïf works by Brazil's best (as well as works by other self-taught painters from around the world) grace the walls of this lovely colonial mansion that was once the studio of painter Eliseu Visconti. The pieces in what is reputedly the world's largest and most complete collection of primitive paintings date from the 15th century through contemporary times. Don't miss the colorful, colossal (7-×4-m/223-×13-ft) canvas that depicts the city of Rio; it reportedly took five years to complete. This museum sprang from a collection started decades ago by a jewelry designer who later created a foundation to oversee the art. A small gift shop sells postcards, T-shirts, and other items. *Rua Cosme Velho 561, Tijuca, tel. 021/2205–8612 or 021/2205–8547. R$5. Tues.–Fri. 10–6, weekends noon–6.*

In This Chapter

Updated by Ana Lúcia do Vale

eating out

MEAT LOVERS WILL BE MESMERIZED by the succulent offerings in Rio's churrascarias, especially those that serve *rodízio* style (grilled meat on skewers is continuously brought to your table—until you can eat no more). Hotel restaurants often offer feijoada on Saturday (sometimes Friday, too). Vegetarians will appreciate the abundance of salad bars, where you pay for your greens by the kilo. And seafood restaurants are in abundance. (Note that it's perfectly safe to eat fresh produce in clean, upscale places; avoid shellfish in all but the best restaurants.)

Cariocas have scaled back on *almoço* (lunch), which used to be a full meal, and have turned more to *lanche* (a sandwich). Dinner is a late affair; if you arrive at 7, you may be the only one in the restaurant. Popular places seat customers until well after midnight on weekends, when the normal closing hour is 2 AM. Cariocas love to linger in *choperias*, plain but pleasant bars that may also serve food, and such establishments abound. Most serve dishes in the $–$$ range, and portions are large enough for two people to share.

SPECIALTIES

Many Brazilian dishes are adaptations of Portuguese specialties. Fish stews called *caldeiradas* and beef stews called *cozidos* (a wide variety of vegetables boiled with different cuts of beef and pork) are popular, as is *bacalhau*, salt cod cooked in sauce or grilled. *Salgados* (literally "salteds") are appetizers or snacks served in sit-down restaurants as well as stand-up *lanchonetes* (luncheonettes). Dried salted meats form the basis of many dishes from the interior and northeast of Brazil, and pork is used heavily in dishes from Minas Gerais. The national dish of Brazil is *feijoada* (a stew of black beans, sausage, pork, and beef), which is often served with arroz, shredded kale, orange slices, and manioc flour or meal—called *farofa* if it's coarsely ground, *farinha* if finely ground—that has been fried with onions, oil, and egg.

Brazilian *doces* (desserts) are very sweet, and many are descendants of the egg-based custards and puddings of Portugal and France. *Cocada* is shredded coconut caked with sugar; *quindim* is a small tart made from egg yolks and coconut; *doce de banana* (or any other fruit) is banana cooked in sugar; ambrosia is a lumpy milk and sugar pudding.

Coffee is served black and strong with sugar in demitasse cups and is called *cafezinho*. (Note that requests for *descafeinado* will be met with a firm shake of the head "no," a blank stare, or outright amusement—it's just not a Brazilian thing.) Coffee is taken with milk—called *café com leite*—only at breakfast. Bottled mineral water is sold in two forms: with and without bubbles (*com gas* and *sem gas*, respectively).

The national drink is the *caipirinha*, made of crushed lime, sugar, and *pinga* or *cachaça* (sugarcane liquor). When whipped with crushed ice, fruit juices, and condensed milk, the pinga/cachaça becomes a *batida*. A *caipivodka*, or *caipiroska*, is the same cocktail with vodka instead of cachaça. Some bars make both drinks using fruit other than lime, like kiwi and *maracujá* (passion fruit). Brazil's best bottled beer is Cerpa, sold at most restaurants. In general, though, Brazilians prefer tap beer, called *chopp*, which is sold by all bars and some restaurants. Be sure to try the carbonated soft drink *guaraná*, made using the Amazonian fruit of the same name.

PRICES AND DRESS

Many restaurants offer a special fixed-price menu as well as à la carte fare. Many also include what is referred to as cover charge for the bread and other appetizers placed on the table. Leaving a 10% tip is enough, but check your bill: the service charge may already have been added. Some restaurants don't accept credit cards, many are closed on Monday, and dress is almost always casual.

CATEGORY	COST*
$$$$	over R$40
$$$	R$30–$40
$$	R$20–R$30
$	R$10–R$20
¢	under R$10

**per person for a dinner entrée*

BRAZILIAN

$$–$$$$ **ESPLANADA GRILL.** This churrascaria serves high-quality meat like T-bone steak (R$29) or picanha, a tasty Brazilian cut of beef marbled with some fat (R$23 half portion). All the grilled dishes come with fried palm hearts, baked potatoes, and rice. Brazilian TV stars like to hang out at this upscale eatery. *Rua Barão da Torre 600, Ipanema, tel. 021/2512–2970. DC, MC, V.*

$$$ **MARIU'S.** This highly regarded churrascaria serves more than a dozen types of sizzling meats, rodízio style (R$32 per person). Right next door, Mario's Crustáceos specializes in seafood. Reservations are a good idea. *Av. Atlântica 290A, Leme, tel. 021/2542–2393. DC, MC, V.*

$$$ ★ **PORCÃO.** Waiters at these quintessential rodízio-style churrascarias fly up and down between rows of linen-draped tables wielding giant skewers laden with sizzling barbecued beef, pork, and chicken. All the branches resonate with the good humor

rio de janeiro dining

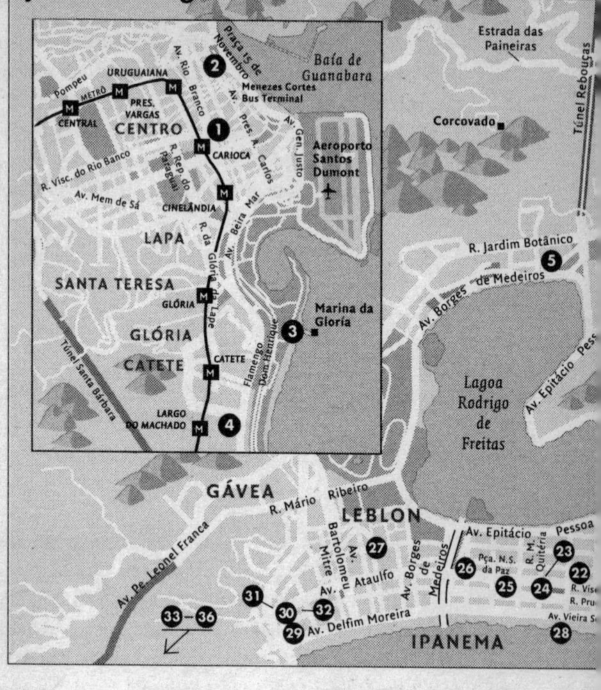

Adega Aragon, 13
Alfredo, 37
Alho & Óleo, 4, 23
Antiquarius, 30
Barra Grill, 33
Bistrô do Paço, 2
Carême, 6
Casa da Feijoada, 18
Celeiro, 31
Cipriani, 12
Claude Troisgros, 5
Colombo, 1
D'Amici, 8
Doce Delícia, 24
Don Camillo, 15
Esplanada Grill, 25
Galani, 28
Garcia & Rodrigues, 32
Garfo Livre, 14
Guapo Loco, 29
Mariu's, 11
Margutta, 26
Monseigneur, 34
Porcão, 3, 21, 35
Quatro Sete Meia, 36

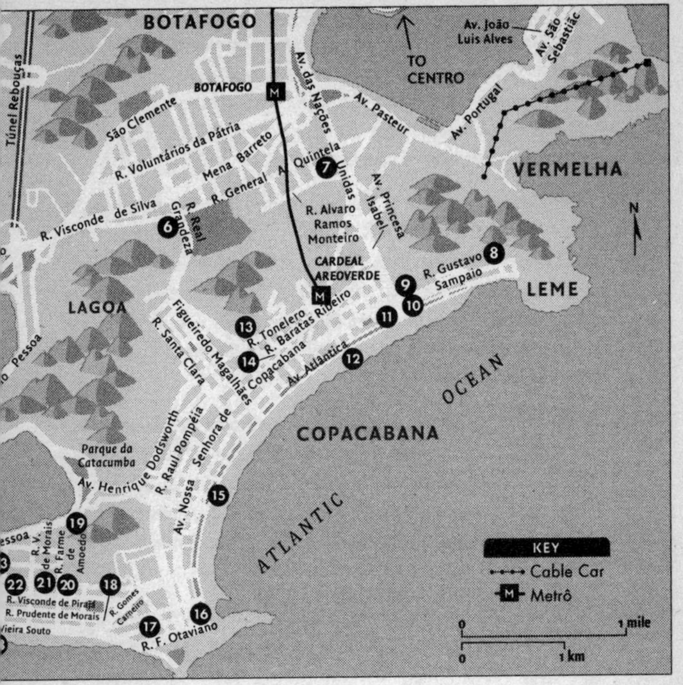

Le Pré-Catalan, 16

Le Saint Honoré, 10

Satyricon, 22

Shirley, 9

Siri Mole, 17

Spices, 19

Terra Brasilius, 27

Yemanjá, 20

Yorubá, 7

that seems to accompany this slightly primitive form of eating. Save room if you can: the papaya creme pudding topped by a bit of cassis shouldn't be missed. *Rua Barão da Torre 218, Ipanema, tel. 021/2522–0999; Av. Armando Lombardi 591, Barra da Tijuca, tel. 021/2492–2001; Av. Infante Dom Henrique, Parque do Flamengo, tel. 021/2554–8862. Reservations not accepted. AE, DC, MC, V.*

$$$ ★ **SIRI MOLE.** If you want to eat typical food from the northeast of Brazil, this is the place. It's a small but absolutely comfortable restaurant that makes exotic dishes, such as *acarajé*, a mix of fried smashed white beans and shrimp. Don't miss the *moqueca de siri*, a hot stew made of crabs, *dendê* oil (a kind of spicy olive oil), and coconut milk. *Rua Francisco Otaviano 50, Copacabana, tel. 021/2267–0894. AE, DC, MC, V.*

$$–$$$ **BARRA GRILL.** Informal and popular, this steak house serves some of the best meat in town and is a favorite stop after a long day at the beach. Prices for the rodízio-style meals are slightly more expensive on weekends than during the week. *Av. Ministro Ivan Lins 314, Barra da Tijuca, tel. 021/2493–6060. Reservations not accepted. AE, DC, MC, V.*

$$–$$$ ★ **YORUBÁ.** The menu reflects owner Neide Santos's origins. A *baiana* (woman from the northeastern Brazilian state of Bahia) by birth, she offers African-Brazilian dishes typical of that region. African sculptures, blue windows, and green leaves spread all over the place, make up the decor. The *piripiri* (a spicy rice with ginger, coconut milk, and shrimp) is worth it at R$65 for two. *Rua Arnaldo Quintela 94, Botafogo, tel. 021/2541–9387. No credit cards.*

$$ ★ **CASA DA FEIJOADA.** Brazil's savory national dish is the specialty here, where huge pots of the stew simmer every day (R$25 per person). The restaurant does a superb job with desserts as well, whipping up a lovely selection of traditional sweets with flavors like banana or pumpkin. To drink, try the caipirinha made with cachaça and not only lime but also other fruits like tangerine, passion fruit, pineapple, strawberry, or kiwi. Be careful though, caipirinha is strong, and the sweet taste can be deceptive. *Rua*

Prudente de Morais 10, Ipanema, tel. 021/2523–4994 or 021/2247–2776. AE, DC, MC, V.

$–$$ TERRA BRASILIS. Large windows overlooking a tree-lined street, cool white-ceramic tile, and stucco walls painted buttercup yellow and celery green give this "weigh-and-pay" restaurant a cheery atmosphere. For lunch, simply help yourself to the Brazilian buffet (including a good selection of salads) and head to a counter, where your plate is weighed. It works out to about R$16 a kilo on weekdays, R$18 on weekends, but it's really hard to eat that much. And, yes, they do take the plate's weight into account. For dinner, the system changes to rodízio-style service of several Brazilian dishes: fried, dried meat, and red and black beans. *Rua Humberto de Campos 699, Leblon, tel. 021/2274–4702, www.cozinhatipica,com.br.* AE, DC, MC, V.

$–$$ YEMANJÁ. Featuring typical food from Bahia, this restaurant serves portions big enough for two. Try the *bobó de camarão*, made of shrimp and mashed *aipim* (a root vegetable similar to potato). For dessert, opt for the white or black *cocada*, a sugar and coconut confection cooked either a short time (white), or a longer time (black). *Rua Visconde de Pirajá 128, Ipanema, tel. 021/2247–7004.* AE, DC, MC, V.

CAFÉS

¢–$$ ★ GARCIA & RODRIGUES. It's a combination café, delicatessen, liquor shop, and trendy restaurant. High-society cariocas breakfast at this expensive but cozy place. At lunchtime, choose from a selection of sandwiches, made with ingredients such as salmon. *Av. Ataulfo de Paiva 1251, Leblon, tel. 021/2512–8188.* AE, DC, MC, V.

¢–$ ★ COLOMBO. At the turn of the 20th century, this belle epoque structure was Rio's preeminent café, the site of afternoon teas for high-society *senhoras* and a center of political intrigue and gossip. Jacaranda-framed mirrors from Belgium and stained glass from France add to the art nouveau decor. Portions are generous, but you can also just stop by for a pastry and coffee while you absorb the opulence. *Rua Gonçalves Dias 32, Centro, tel. 021/2232–2300. Reservations not accepted. No credit cards. Closed Sun. No dinner. Metrô: Carioca.*

ECLECTIC

$$$–$$$$ **SPICES.** A Caribbean flair presides over the creative menu here. An extensive array of mixed drinks includes the Nêga Sings the Blues (a variation of the caipirinha made with cachaça, lime, ginger, and honey). The entrées have similarly offbeat names, and many of the seafood, fowl, and meat dishes employ fruits and nuts in their preparation. Try the ginger tuna with mango or the grilled beef with Gorgonzola and pumpkin purée. Spices has some of the best-looking salads in town as well. *Av. Epitácio Pessoa 864, Lagoa, tel. 021/2259–1041. AE.*

$–$$$$ ★ **ALHO & ÓLEO.** On Ipanema's Praça Nossa Senhora da Paz, this restaurant features an eclectic menu with a hint of Italy. Interesting fowl dishes include partridge with dates and grilled duck with apricots; the arugula salad with eggplant, mushrooms, and sea bass is also recommended. Homemade pasta dishes include a farfalle with seafood and artichokes. *Rua Barão da Torre 348, Ipanema, tel. 021/2247–6711 or 021/2247–6712; Rua Buarque de Macedo 13, Flamengo, tel. 021/2225–3418. AE.*

$ **GARFO LIVRE.** The by-the-kilo buffets at this eatery two blocks from the beach give economical eating a new twist. As you enter, you're given a card on which the items you select are marked. Grab a plate, help yourself to the buffet—which has many Middle Eastern dishes—get your plate weighed, and then pay on your way out. The salad bar has a large selection that includes beans, hummus, and steamed and raw veggies. Commuters come on weeknights beginning at 7—trading rush hour for happy hour. *Av. Nossa Senhora de Copacabana 1003, Copacabana, tel. 021/3813–5571. AE, DC, MC, V.*

FRENCH

$$$$ **CARÊME.** The R$70 prix-fixe menu here includes a choice of some ★ of the best French desserts in town. *Delícia de limão* (lemon delicacy) is a must-try. It's made of several thin layers of a hazelnut biscuit lightly soaked with lemon juice and stacked with honey mousse and lemon cream; atop it all are merengue, small pieces of white chocolate, and a strawberry. *Rua Visconde de Caravelas 113, Botafogo, tel. 021/2537–5431. Reservations essential. No lunch. DC, MC.*

$$$$ **LE PRÉ-CATALAN.** In the hotel Sofitel Rio Palace is a carioca version of the charming Parisian restaurant of the same name in the Bois du Boulogne. Reopened in 1998 with chef Roland Villard, this has become one of the best French restaurants in Rio. Every two weeks it has a new prix-fixe menu (R$65 with three choices for appetizers, main dish, and a dessert). *Av. Atlântica 4240, Level E, Copacabana, tel. 021/2525–1160. Reservations essential. AE, DC, MC, V. No lunch.*

$$$$ **LE SAINT HONORÉ.** Le Saint Honoré offers diners French cuisine and an extraordinary view of Copacabana Beach from atop Le Meridien hotel. Brazilian fruits and herbs tucked into dishes produce such gems as *les pièces du boucher marquées sauces gamay et béarnaise*, a fillet with both béarnaise and red-wine sauces. A jacket and tie are advised. *Av. Atlântica 1020, 37th floor, Copacabana, tel. 021/3873–8880. Reservations essential. AE, DC, MC, V.*

$$$–$$$$ **CLAUDE TROISGROS.** Many consider this Rio's finest restaurant. ★ The menu is famed for nouvelle cuisine relying entirely on Brazilian ingredients. Every dish—from the crab or lobster flan to chicken, fish, and duck prepared with exotic herbs and sauces—is pure pleasure and always exceptionally light. The dessert menu is headed by a to-die-for passion-fruit mousse. *Rua Custódio Serrão 62, Jardim Botânico, tel. 021/2537–8582. Reservations essential. AE, DC.*

$$–$$$$ **MONSEIGNEUR.** Modern and traditional French cuisine meet here, where the grand decor matches the meals—two striking lighted columns of translucent crystal dominate the center of the restaurant. The disadvantage is that to get to the Inter-Continental Rio hotel you'll need a cab. *Av. Prefeito Mendes de Morais 222, São Conrado, tel. 021/3323–2200. Reservations essential. AE, DC, MC, V. No lunch.*

ITALIAN

$$$–$$$$ **CIPRIANI.** The Copacabana Palace hotel's restaurant offers a superb dining experience. Start with a Cipriani—champagne with fresh peach juice (really a Bellini). The snook carpaccio with apple and fennel is a marvelous appetizer; so is the salad of endive marinated in red wine. The pastas must be imported from heaven, and the meat and fish entrées are, appropriate to their lavish surroundings, fit for kings. None of this, of course, comes cheaply. *Av. Atlântica 1702, Copacabana, tel. 021/2545–8747. Reservations essential. AE, DC, MC, V.*

$$–$$$$ ★ **MARGUTTA.** A good wine list complements the cuisine here. The pasta, fish, and risottos are all top drawer—and always fresh. *Av. Henrique Dumont 62, Ipanema, tel. 021/2511–0878. AE, DC, V. No lunch weekdays.*

$–$$$$ **D'AMICI.** This restaurant is a pleasant surprise formed from the collaboration of two maître d's, Antonio Salustiano and Candido Alves, and a sommelier, Walmir Pereira. None of the three is Italian; in fact, they all come from the northeast of Brazil. But the lamb with rice and herbs is divine, and the boar meat with red wine sauce is irresistible. Many dishes aren't listed on the fixed menu—ask for suggestions. *Rua Antônio Vieira 18, Leme, tel. 021/2541–4477. AE, DC, MC, V.*

$$–$$$ **ALFREDO.** The mainstay is the pasta, especially the fettuccine Alfredo. Start your meal with a selection from the ample cold buffet of antipasti, which may include traditional pastas served with a variety of sauces. The restaurant is in the Inter-Continental hotel and has a view of the pool area. *Av. Prefeito Mendes de Morais 222, São Conrado, tel. 021/3323–2200. AE, DC, MC, V. No lunch.*

MEXICAN

$–$$ **GUAPO LOCO.** The bustling crowds feast on tamales, enchiladas, and other Mexican favorites until closing time at 3 AM. Tequila has garnered quite a following among the young; the margaritas are good. *Rua Rainha Guilhermina 48, Leblon, tel. 021/2294–2915. AE, DC, MC, V. No lunch weekdays.*

PORTUGUESE

$$–$$$$ ★ **ADEGA ARAGON.** Simple, but original, this restaurant has more than 20 kinds of *bacalhau* (cod) on the menu. There's also the *sinfonia marítima* (R$38 for two), a grilled seafood medley of shrimp, squid, and fresh fish served with rice. *Rua Siqueira Campos 18B, Copacabana, tel. 021/2257–1427. AE, D, DC, MC, V.*

$$–$$$$ ★ **ANTIQUARIUS.** This much-loved establishment is as famous for its flawless—and award-winning—rendering of Portuguese classics as for its high prices. Wander through the antiques shop at the restaurant before settling in at a table. A recommended dish is the *cozido*, a stew with a multitude of ingredients, including bananas. The *cataplana*, a seafood stew with rice, is also marvelous, and the *perna de cordeiro* (leg of lamb) is the most requested dish on the menu. The wine list impresses even Portuguese gourmets. *Rua Aristides Espínola 19, Leblon, tel. 021/2294–1049. Reservations essential. DC.*

SEAFOOD

$$$$ **GALANI.** Although it overlooks action-packed Ipanema, the mood at this Caesar Park hotel restaurant is quiet. The buffet (R$43 weekdays, R$59 weekends) has everything from salads and seafood to pasta and carpaccio. *Av. Antônio Carlos Jobim 460, Ipanema, tel. 021/2525–2525. AE, DC, MC, V.*

$$$–$$$$ ★ **SATYRICON.** This eclectic Italian seafood restaurant, which also has a branch in Búzios, is rumored to have been Madonna's

favorite eatery when she was in town. The *pargo* (fish baked in a thick layer of rock salt) is a specialty, and the sushi and sashimi are well loved. It's expensive, but it has some of the best seafood in town. *Rua Barão da Torre 192, Ipanema, tel. 021/2521–0627. DC, MC, V.*

$–$$$$ ★ **SHIRLEY.** Homemade Spanish seafood casseroles and soups are the draw at this traditional Copacabana restaurant tucked onto a shady street. Try the *zarzuela*, a seafood soup, or *cazuela*, a fish fillet with white-wine sauce. Don't be turned off by the simple decor (a few paintings hung on wood-paneled walls): the food is terrific. *Rua Gustavo Sampaio 610, Leme, tel. 021/2275–1398. Reservations not accepted. No credit cards.*

$–$$$ ★ **DON CAMILLO.** There's always something new on the menu at this Copacabana beachfront restaurant. Try the fried seafood platter (R$22) with shrimp, sardines, and fresh fish of the day. The Italian atmosphere is completed by a musical group that sings traditional songs. *Av. Atlântica 3056, Copacabana, tel. 021/2549–9958, www.tempero.com.br. AE, D, DC, MC, V.*

$–$$$ ★ **QUATRO SETE MEIA.** Internationally renowned, this restaurant is one hour by car west of Copacabana, at the end of a highway that offers stunning coastal views. Simplicity is the soul of the restaurant—whose name is its street number—and the village in which it's set. There are only 11 tables: five indoors and six in a garden at water's edge. The menu carries seven delicious options, including *moquecas* (seafood stews), grilled seafood, and curries. *Rua Barros de Alarcão 476, Pedra da Guaratiba, tel. 021/2417–1716. Reservations essential. No credit cards. Closed Mon.–Tues. No dinner Wed.–Thurs.*

VEGETARIAN

$$$ **CELEIRO.** What may be Rio's sole organic restaurant is always full for lunch. The buffet offers approximately 40 salads as well as a wide selection of pastas for R$33 per kilo. *Rua Dias Ferreira 199, Leblon, tel. 021/2274–7843. D, MC, V. No dinner.*

¢–$ **BISTRÔ DO PAÇO.** A good option for a light lunch, the daily buffet of salads (R$9 per person) includes carrot salad with oranges, potatoes, and apples. For R$10 you can try also an onion, cheese, or spinach quiche. *Praça Quinze 48, Centro, tel. 021/2262–3613. MC, V. No dinner.*

¢–$ **DOCE DELÍCIA.** Make your own salad by choosing 5 to 15 of the 42 items offered daily. Dressings run the gamut from light and yogurt-based to innovative, with mustard and lemon. A large portion is R$11, a small R$9. *Rua Aníbal de Mendonça 55, Ipanema, tel. 021/2259–0239. V.*

In This Chapter

Updated by Ana Lúcia do Vale

shopping

FROM SOPHISTICATED JEWELRY AND EURO-STYLE CLOTHES to teeny tangas and funky tie-dyed dresses, the selection is broad. You can stroll down streets lined with fashionable boutiques, barter with vendors at street fairs, or wander through one of more than two dozen air-conditioned malls. Good bets include leather, suede, jewelry, and cool summer clothing in natural fibers—appropriate for the climate. Also look for coffee, samba and bossa nova CDs, and art. (Note that larger shoe sizes, once difficult to find in Rio, are now common.)

Ipanema is Rio's most fashionable shopping district. Its many exclusive boutiques are in arcades, with the majority along Rua Visconde de Pirajá. In Copacabana you'll find souvenir shops, bookstores, and branches of some of Rio's better shops along Avenida Nossa Senhora de Copacabana and the streets just off it. If upscale jewelry catches your fancy, head for Avenida Atlântica.

Brazil is one of the world's largest producers of gold and the largest supplier of colored gemstones, with important deposits of aquamarines, amethysts, diamonds, emeralds, rubellites, topazes, and tourmalines. To get an idea of what's available, figure out what stones interest you and compare their quality and price at various shops. If you're planning to go to Minas Gerais, save your jewelry shopping for there; otherwise, stick with shops that offer certificates of authenticity and quality.

CENTERS AND MALLS

BARRA SHOPPING (Av. das Américas 4666, Barra da Tijuca, tel. 021/2431–9922) is one of South America's largest complexes. Although it's slightly out of the way, shoppers from all over town head for this mall, which features a medical center, eight movie theaters, and a bowling alley as well as shops.

NEW YORK CITY CENTER (Av. das Américas 5000, Barra da Tijuca, tel. 021/2432–4980), just beside Barra Shopping, is one of the newest in town, easily recognizable by the enormous replica of the Statue of Liberty that hangs out front. There are 18 movie theaters, the nightclub Studio 54, upscale restaurants, and Gameworks—where you can play with flying simulators. The best way to reach Barra da Tijuca is by car or by taxi (R$50 roundtrip). But there's also the CityRio bus.

RIO OFF PRICE SHOPPING (Rua General Severiano 97, Botafogo, tel. 021/2542–5693), just down the street from the Rio Sul shopping center, is a mall with prices 20% lower than usual. The complex has snack bars and two movie theaters.

RIO SUL (Av. Lauro Müller 116, Botafogo, tel. 021/2295–1332) is one of the city's most popular retail complexes, with more than 400 shops. The shopping is sophisticated, and the food court is endless.

SÃO CONRADO FASHION MALL (Estrada da Gávea 899, São Conrado, tel. 021/3322–0300) sells a wide array of international and domestic fashions and is Rio's most appealing mall, as it's the least crowded and has an abundance of natural light.

SHOPPING CENTER CASSINO ATLÂNTICO (Av. Nossa Senhora de Copacabana, Copacabana, tel. 021/2247–8709), adjoining the Rio Palace hotel, is dominated by antiques shops, jewelry stores, art galleries, and souvenir outlets.

SHOPPING CENTER DA GÁVEA (Rua Marquês de São Vicente 52, Gávea, tel. 021/2274–9896) has a small but select mix of fashionable clothing and leather goods stores. It also has several top art galleries, of which the best are Ana Maria Niemeyer, Beco da Arte, Borghese, Bronze, Paulo Klabin, Saramenha, and Toulouse.

VIA PARQUE (Av. Ayrton Senna 3000, Barra da Tijuca, tel. 021/3385–0100) is a 230-store complex popular for its outlets and ample parking (nearly 2,000 spaces). In addition to movie theaters and fast-food restaurants, the mall is home to the ATL Hall Theater.

MARKETS

The **FEIRA HIPPIE** is a colorful handicrafts street fair held every Sunday 9–6 in Ipanema's Praça General Osório. Offerings run the gamut from jewelry and hand-painted dresses and T-shirts to paintings and wood carvings, leather bags and sandals, rag dolls, knickknacks, and even furniture. A handful of booths sells samba percussion instruments.

In the evenings and on weekends along the median of **AVENIDA ATLÂNTICA,** artisans spread out their wares. You'll find paintings, carvings, handicrafts, sequined dresses, and hammocks from the northeast. Saturday (during daylight hours) an open-air fair near the **PRAÇA 15 DE NOVEMBRO** has such goods as china and silver sets, watches, Asian rugs, and chandeliers. Vendors at **RIO ANTIQUE FAIR,** on Rua do Lavradio in Centro, sell antiques, rare books, records, and all types of objets d'art on Saturday afternoon. The antiques sellers move to the **CASA SHOPPING CENTER,** in Barra da Tijuca, on Sunday.

The crowded, lively **FEIRA NORDESTINA** (Northeastern Fair), held every Sunday 6–1 at the Campo de São Cristóvão, is a social event for northeasterners living in Rio. They gather to hear their own distinctive music, eat regional foods, and buy tools and cheap clothing.

BABILÔNIA FEIRA HYPE (tel. 021/2253-9800 or 021/2263-7667, www.babiloniahype.com.br) opens weekends from 3–11 every fortnight inside the Jóquei Club Brasileiro, at Rua Jardim Botânico. This fair brings together fashion, design, art, and gastronomy. It's not only good for shopping, but for watching the beautiful people go by. Admission is R$3, but it's free for children under eight.

SPECIALTY SHOPS

Art

BONINO (Rua Barata Ribeiro 578, Copacabana, tel. 021/2294-7810) has been around for some 30 years, and is the most traditional, best known, and most visited of Rio's art galleries.

COHN EDELSTEIN (Rua Jangadeira 14B, Ipanema, tel. 021/2523-0549; Rua Barão da Torre 185A, Ipanema, tel. 021/2287-9933) is an internationally respected contemporary art gallery showing Brazilian works.

CONTORNO (Shopping Center da Gávea, Rua Marquês de São Vicente 52, Gávea, tel. 021/2274-3832) hosts an eclectic gallery, but the art it displays is certainly Brazilian.

RIO DESIGN CENTER (Av. Ataulfo de Paiva 270, Leblon, tel. 021/2274-7893) contains several galleries, including Borghese, Beco da Arte, Montesanti, Museum, and Way.

Beachwear

BLUEMAN (Rio Sul, Av. Lauro Müller 116, Botafogo, tel. 021/2220-4898), a bikini shop with many mall locations in addition to the Rio Sul branch, carries the bathing suits–tangas—that virtually define Brazil in much of North America's imagination. Tangas are said to have been invented in Ipanema—and they don't take up much room in your luggage.

BUM BUM (Rua Vinicius de Moraes 130, Ipanema, tel. 021/2521–1229) is the market leader in beachwear, with locations in Rio Sul and Barra Shopping in addition to its Ipanema branch.

SALINAS (Forum de Ipanema, Visconde de Pirajá 351, Ipanema), a *très* chic bikini designer, is the label de rigueur with the fashionable in Búzios and other resort areas.

CDs

TOCA DO VINÍCIUS (Rua Vinicius de Moraes 129, Ipanema, tel. 021/2247–5227) bills itself as a "cultural space and bossa nova salon." The shop, though tiny, does indeed seem like a gathering place for bossa-nova aficionados from around the world (if you're one of them, there's a good chance you'll leave the shop with an e-mail address for at least one new pal). Amid the atmosphere of bonhomie, you'll find books (a few in English), sheet music, and T-shirts as well as CDs.

Clothing

ALICE TAPAJÓS (Fórum de Ipanema, Visconde de Pirajá 351, Ipanema, tel. 021/2247–2594) carries DKNY and other well-known sportswear in its Ipanema, São Conrado Fashion Mall, and Barra Shopping locations.

AR LIVRE (Av. Nossa Senhora de Copacabana 900, Copacabana, tel. 021/2549–8994) has an exceptional selection of good quality T-shirts and beachwear at appealing prices.

KRISHNA (Rio Sul, Av. Lauro Müller 116, Botafogo, tel. 021/2542–2443; São Conrado Fashion Mall, Estrada da Gávea 899, São Conrado, tel. 021/3322–0437) specializes in classic feminine dresses and separates—many in fine linens, cottons, and silks.

LOJAS AMERICANAS (Rua do Passeio 42–56, Centro, tel. 021/2524–0138), Rio's largest chain department store, focuses on mostly casual fashions for men, women, and children. But it also has a wide selection of toys, records, cosmetics, and sporting goods.

Handicrafts

CASA DO PEQUENO EMPRESÁRIO (Rua Real Grandeza 293, Botafogo, tel. 021/2286–9464) is an exposition center for handcrafted items made of everything from porcelain to wood and papier-mâché to clay.

FOLCLORE (Rua Visconde de Pirajá 490, Ipanema, tel. 021/2259–7442). This handicrafts shop bursts with primitive paintings, costume jewelry, leather and ceramic crafts, and birds and flowers carved from stone. Quality is high, but take note: some items have been imported from other South American nations.

Jewelry

AMSTERDAM SAUER (Rua Visconde de Pirajá 484, Ipanema, tel. 021/2512–9878) is one of Rio's top names in jewelry, with top prices, to boot. Jules Roger Sauer, the founder of these stores (with branches in Brazil, the United States, and the Caribbean), is particularly known for his fascination with emeralds. The on-site gemstone museum (tel. 021/2239–8045) is open weekdays 10–5 and Saturday 9:30–1 (tour reservations are a good idea).

ANTÔNIO BERNARDO (Gávea, Forum Ipanema, and Fashion Mall shopping malls) has been making gorgeous jewelry with contemporary designs for nearly 30 years.

H. STERN (Rua Visconde de Pirajá 490, Ipanema, tel. 021/2259–7442) is owned by the eponymous Hans Stern, who started his empire in 1945 with an initial investment of about $200. Today his interests include mining and production operations as well as 170 stores in Europe, the Americas, and the Middle East. His award-winning designers create truly distinctive contemporary pieces (the inventory runs to about 300,000 items). At H. Stern world headquarters you can see exhibits of rare stones and watch craftspeople transform rough stones into sparkling jewels. There's also a museum you can tour (by appointment only). If you feel the prices are too high in the upstairs salons, there are shops downstairs that sell more affordable pieces as well as folkloric items.

Leather Goods

BOTTEGA VENETA (Shopping Center da Gávea, Rua Marquês de São Vicente 52, Gávea, tel. 021/2274–8248) has fine women's shoes and bags.

FORMOSINHO (Av. Nossa Senhora de Copacabana 582, Copacabana, tel. 021/2287–8998) sells men's and women's shoes at low, wholesale prices. In addition to its Copacabana location, it has three other stores along Ipanema's Rua Visconde de Pirajá.

FRANKIE AMAURY (Shopping Center da Gávea, Rua Marquês de São Vicente 52, Gávea, tel. 021/2294–8895) is *the* name in leather clothing.

MARIAZINHA (Forum de Ipanema, Praça Nossa Senhora da Paztel, Ipanema, tel. 021/2541–6695) carries fashionable footwear.

NAZARÉ (Shopping Center da Gávea, Rua Marquês de São Vicente 52, Gávea, tel. 021/2294–9849) has bags and fine women's shoes.

VICTOR HUGO (Rio Sul, Av. Lauro Müller 116, Botafogo, tel. 021/2275–3388) carries women's handbags.

In This Chapter

Updated by Ana Lúcia do Vale

outdoor activities and sports

THE JOY FOR LIFE and excellent weather make Rio a great place for sport: you can sail the ocean, run along the city's boulevards, or hang glide off the mountainside. When you're ready to have a seat, check out one of Rio's exciting auto races or an impassioned *futebol* (soccer) game.

PARTICIPANT SPORTS

Bicycling and Running

Bikers and runners share the boulevards along the beach and, for cooler and quieter outings, the path around Lagoa Rodrigo de Freitas. On weekends many cariocas also bike or run along the stretch of Floresta da Tijuca Road that becomes pedestrians only. Although hotels can arrange bike rentals, it's just as easy to rent from stands along beachfront avenues or the road ringing the lagoon. Rates are about R$10 per hour. You're usually asked to show identification and give your hotel name and room number, but deposits are seldom required. (Note that helmets aren't usually available.)

Boating and Sailing

CAPTAIN'S YACHT CHARTERS (Rua Conde de Lages 44, Glória, tel. 021/2224–0313) charters all types of crewed vessels for any length of time. You can arrange an afternoon of water-skiing with a speedboat or a weekend aboard a yacht.

Golf

If you're staying at the Sheraton, Inter-Continental, Copacabana Palace, or Rio Atlântica, you get a R$50 discount on the R$150 greens fee at the 18-hole **GÁVEA GOLF CLUB** (Estrada da Gávea 800, São Conrado, tel. 021/3322–4141). Golf lessons run R$30 per half hour. You can rent equipment for the par 3, six-hole greens of the **GOLDEN GREEN GOLF CLUB** (Av. Canal de Marapendi 2901, Barra da Tijuca, tel. 021/2433–3950). But you have to be invited by a club member to have lessons or play at the nine-hole course.

Hang Gliding

At **JUST FLY** (tel. 021/2268–0565) a 30-minute hang glider flight—jumping from Pedra Bonita in the Parque Nacional da Tijuca, and landing at Praia do Pepino in São Conrado—costs approximately R$170 including transportation to and from your hotel. For a little more, you can have 12 pictures taken as well. **SUPERFLY** (Estrada das Canoas 1476, Casa 2, São Conrado, tel. 021/3332–2286) offers hang-gliding classes and tandem flights with instructors. A package including pick-up at your hotel and 12 photos taken in-flight costs about R$220.

Hiking

CENTRO EXCURSIONISTA BRASILEIRO (Av. Almirante Barroso 2–8, Centro, tel. 021/2252–9844) provides guides, maps, and gear for hiking expeditions throughout the metropolitan area.

Tennis

There are nine courts for rent at **FAZENDA CLUBE MARAPENDI** (Av. das Américas 3979, Barra da Tijuca, tel. 021/3325–2440). The large, well-equipped health club **RIO SPORT CENTER** (Av. Ayrton Senna 2541, Barra da Tijuca, tel. 021/3325–6644) has six tennis courts (three covered). Court time runs from R$16–R$69 per hour depending on whether you want to play in the morning or at night on the covered courts. You can also rent equipment and arrange lessons.

SPECTATOR SPORTS

Auto Racing

Brazilian race-car drivers rank among the world's best and frequently compete in international events. You'll get a taste of the speed if you watch the checkered flag drop on competitions in the Formula I Grand Prix circuit named after one of the country's most famous racers, Emerson Fittipaldi. The racetrack is the **AUTÓDROMO INTERNACIONAL NELSON PIQUET** (Av. Embaixador Abelardo Bueno, Jacarepagua, tel. 021/2441–2158).

Futebol

You can watch a match at the **ESTÁDIO MARACANÃ** (Rua Prof. Eurico Rabelo, Maracanã, tel. 021/2264–9962). The fans are half the spectacle. During the season the top game is played each Sunday at around 5 PM. The three most popular teams are Flamengo, Fluminense, and Vasco da Gama. Play between any of them is soccer at its finest.

Horse Racing

Races are held year-round in the **JÓQUEI CLUBE** (Praça Santos Dumont 31, Gávea, tel. 021/2512–9988) beginning Monday and Thursday at 7 PM and weekends at noon. The big event of the year, the Brazilian Derby, is held the first Sunday of August.

In This Chapter

Updated by Ana Lúcia do Vale

nightlife and the arts

RIO'S NIGHTLIFE IS AS HARD TO RESIST as its beaches. Options range from samba shows shamelessly aimed at visitors to sultry dance halls that play *forró*, a music style that originated in Brazil's northeast during World War II. (American GIs stationed at refueling stops opened up their clubs "for all," which, when pronounced with a Brazilian accent, became "forró.") You'll find spots that feature the sounds of big band, rock, and everything in between. One of the happiest mediums is *música popular brasileira* (MPB), the generic term for popular Brazilian music, which ranges from pop to jazz. Note that establishments in this carefree city often have carefree hours; call ahead to confirm opening times.

There are also many performing arts options, including opera, theater, music, dance, and film. For current listings, pick up the bilingual *Rio Guia*, published by Riotur, the city's tourist board; *Este Mês no Rio/This Month in Rio* and similar publications are available at most hotels, and your hotel concierge is also a good source of information. The Portuguese-language newspapers *Jornal do Brasil* and *O Globo* both publish schedules of events in the entertainment sections of their Friday editions.

NIGHTLIFE

Bars, Choperias, and Lounges

Bars and lounges often ask for a nominal cover in the form of either a drink minimum or a music charge. Choperias attract an unattached crowd looking for an ice-cold Brazilian draft beer.

BAR BOFETADA. Downstairs the tables flow out onto the street; upstairs large windows open to the sky and afford a good view of the action below. The young, energetic crowd downs chopp and caipirinhas and delicious seafood (the owners are Portuguese) or meat platters large enough to share. *Rua Farme de Amoedo 87–87A, Ipanema, tel. 021/2523–3992 or 021/5523–3992.*

BAR GAROTA DE IPANEMA. The choperia where regulars Tom Jobim and Vinicius de Moraes, authors of *The Girl from Ipanema*, sat and longingly watched the song's heroine head for the beach. (See if you can guess where they usually sat. Hint: it's a table for two near a door.) *Rua Vinicius de Moraes 39, Ipanema, tel. 021/2267–5757.*

BARRIL 1800. An unpretentious beachfront choperia, this Ipanema landmark is usually jammed with people grabbing an icy beer or cocktail and a snack. *Av. Antônio Carlos Jobim 110, Ipanema, tel. 021/2287–0085.*

BRACARENSE. Don't expect to find fancy people in this small, informal place where cariocas linger with their beer on the sidewalk in front of the bar. It's perfect for after a soccer game in Maracanã; many just go there to talk about sports. *Rua José Linhares 85B, Leblon, tel. 021/2294–3549.*

CERVANTES. The chopp here goes well with the meat-and-pineapple combo dishes for which Cervantes is famous. *Av. Prado Júnior 335, Copacabana, tel. 021/2275–6174.*

CHICO'S BAR. Owned by nightspot entrepreneur Chico Recarey, both the bar and the adjoining restaurant, Castelo da Lagoa, are big with affluent carioca singles and couples. *Av. Epitácio Pessoa 1560, Lagoa, tel. 021/2523–3514.*

HIPÓDROMO. Good chopp, honest food, and many young, happy people are the norm at this bar near the Jóquei Clube. *Praça Santos Dumont, Gávea, tel. 021/2294–0095.*

JAZZMANIA. If you arrive before nightfall, you get a superb view of Ipanema Beach at sunset from one of the better jazz clubs in town. *Av. Rainha Elizabeth 769, Ipanema, tel. 021/2227–2447.*

MISTURA FINA. Fine jazz combines with excellent food at Mistura Fina, which is open from midnight to 3 AM. *Av. Borges de Medeiros 3207, Lagoa Rodrigo de Freitas, Lagoa, tel. 021/2537–2844.*

Cybercafés

CYBER PLACE. Plenty of terminals, snacks, and a zippy connection make this the best place to get your E-mail. You'll pay about R$8 per hour, and access is available Monday to Saturday from noon until 2 AM, Sunday from noon to midnight. Cyber Place is in an entertainment complex at the very top of the Rio Sul shopping center. *Av. Lauro Müller 116, Loja D91, Botafogo, tel. 021/2541–1006.*

INTERNET HOUSE. A peaceful place, one block from Copacabana Beach, Internet House has 12 computers, laser and deskjet color printers, and fax and scanner services available. You'll pay about R$10 per hour; access is available Monday–Saturday from 9 AM until 10 PM. *Av. Nossa Senhora de Copacabana 195, Shop 106, Copacabana, tel. 021/2542–3348.*

TUDO É FÁCIL ESTAÇÃO INTERNET. Access is available Monday–Saturday from 10–10 and Sunday from 3–9; you'll pay about R$3 per 15 minutes. *Rua Xavier da Silveira, 19B, Copacabana, tel. 021/2522–3970; Rua Prado Júnior 78, Copacabana, tel. 021/2543–7229.*

Dance Clubs

Rio's *danceterias* (discos) offer flashing lights and loud music. At a number of places, including samba clubs, you can dance to live Brazilian music. *Gafieiras* are old-fashioned ballroom dance halls, usually patronized by an equally old-fashioned clientele.

Upon entry to some clubs you're given a card to carry—each successive drink is marked on it. You pay on departure for what you've consumed.

ASA BRANCA. The decor combines modern geometric designs with old-fashioned fixtures at Chico Recarey's large nightclub. Big bands and popular Brazilian musicians keep the crowd moving until dawn. *Av. Mem de Sá 17, Lapa, tel. 021/2252–4428.*

BALLROOM. Wear your most comfortable clothes—Bermudas and sandals or sundresses—to dance forró here on Thursday. It also hosts concerts, so check which band is playing. *Rua Humaitá 110, Humaitá, tel. 021/2537–7600.*

B.A.S.E. Be prepared for loud music and modern people. The expensive but fashionable B.A.S.E. club is conveniently located near Copacabana Beach. *Rua Francisco Otaviano 20A, Copacabana, tel. 021/2522–0544.*

BIBLO'S BAR. This is *the* place for live music and dancing, particularly if you're single and more than 45 years old. *Av. Epitácio Pessoa 1484, Lagoa, tel. 021/2521–2645.*

DABLIÜBAR. As it's always crowded, you should arrive early, around 10 PM, or after 2 AM. Fancy youngsters fill the place (capacity 550) in between those hours. *Rua Visconde de Pirajá 22, Ipanema, tel. 021/2523–0302.*

EL TURF. A hot spot with a cool location in the Jóquei Clube, the large dance space often fills up with the young and the beautiful. *Praça Santos Dumont 31, Gávea, tel. 021/2274–1444.*

ESTUDANTINA. Opened as a dance hall in 1932, this has become an eternally popular nightclub. On weekends, it packs in as many as 1,500 people. *Praça Tiradentes 79, Centro, tel. 021/2232–1149.*

HARD ROCK CAFE. Even in Rio you can find this megachain outlet in the Shopping Center América. As at other branches, such as in New York or Cannes, you can find huge burgers and beautiful people. *Av. das Américas, 700, 3rd floor, Barra da Tijuca, tel. 021/2232–1149.*

MÉLI MÉLO. A place where fashionable 18- to 25-year-olds go, Méli Mélo is a huge nightclub with two dance floors (one DJ plays '70s music; the other, hip hop and techno). There's also a Japanese restaurant and a cybercafé on-site. *Av. Borges de Medeiros 1426, Lagoa, tel. 021/2219–3132.*

STUDIO 54. In the New York City Center shopping mall is a copy of the disco that was really hot in 1970s Manhattan. The original is gone, but here you can dance all night in one of the most modern, newest, and coolest places in Rio. Be prepared: the DJs play the electronic music really loud. *Av. das Américas 5000, Stores 114–115, Barra da Tijuca, tel. 021/3325–1874.*

SÔBRE AS ONDAS. Dance to live music, usually MPB or samba, overlooking Copacabana Beach. The crowd is mostly over 35. You can also dine at the Terraço Atlântico restaurant, downstairs. *Av. Atlântica 3432, Copacabana, tel. 021/2521–1296.*

Gay and Lesbian Clubs

Rio is a relatively gay-friendly city; the community even has its own gala during Carnaval. Style Travel Agency offers tours targeted to gay and lesbian travelers, and has information on local happenings.

The hippest cariocas—both gay and straight—hang out in Ipanema and Leblon.

BAR DO HOTEL (Av. Delfim Moreira 630, Leblon, tel. 021/2540–4990) is inside the hotel Marina Palace. It serves lunch and dinner, but gets really crowded for drinks on Friday and Saturday nights. The **GALERIA CAFÉ** (Rua Teixeira de Mello, 31 E–F, Ipanema, tel. 021/2523–8250) is a bar with house/techno music for sophisticated gays. From Thursday to Saturday it's not only crowded inside, patrons overflow out onto the sidewalk. Drink minimum is R$10. **LE BOY** (Rua Paul Pompéia 94, Copacabana, tel. 021/2521–0367) is a gay disco that draws an upscale crowd. If you prefer to be where the trends are set, **oo** (Av. Padre Leonel Franca, 240, Gávea, tel. 021/2540–8041) is a new restaurant–café–sushi bar with a dance floor. It's open from 7 PM until 1 PM, but the coffee shop operates 24 hours.

Nightclubs

Although nightclubs often serve food, their main attraction is live music; it's best to eat elsewhere earlier.

If you're interested in entertainment of a steamier variety, stroll along Avenida Princesa Isabel at the end of Copacabana—near Le Meridien hotel—to one of the numerous burlesque, striptease, and sex shows. Be warned, some of the female patrons may be prostitutes.

CANECÃO. Seating up to 5,000 people at tiny tables in a cavernous space, this is the city's largest nightclub, the logical place for some of the biggest names on the international music scene to hold concerts. Reserve a table up front. *Av. Venceslau Brâs 215, Botafogo, tel. 021/2543–1241.*

PLATAFORMA. The most spectacular of Rio's samba shows has elaborate costumes and a variety of musical numbers including samba and rumba. A two-hour show costs about $38.50, drinks not included. Downstairs is a hangout for many local luminaries and entertainers. Upstairs you can eat at Plataforma's famed barbecue restaurant. *Rua Adalberto Ferreira 32, Leblon, tel. 021/2274–4022.*

VINICIUS. You may rightly associate sultry bossa nova with Brazil, but it's increasingly hard to find venues that offer it. This club is one. Along with nightly live samba, jazz, popular music, or bossa nova music, this club has a good kitchen. *Rua Vinicius de Moraes 39, Ipanema, tel. 021/2287–1497.*

THE ARTS

Although MPB may have overshadowed *música erudita* (classical music), Rio has a number of orchestras. The Orquestra Sinfônica Brasileira and the Orquestra do Teatro Municipal are the most prominent. Tickets to performing arts events are inexpensive by international standards and may be purchased at the theater or concert hall box offices. Dress is generally smart casual, although the conservative upper crust still likes to dress elegantly for the Teatro Municipal. Just don't wear valuable jewelry or carry lots of cash.

Rio has an avid film-going public and a well-regarded film industry (you may catch a flick that later hits the international movie circuit). Films are screened in small *cineclubes*, or state-of-the-art movie theaters (many in shopping malls). Foreign movies are shown in their original language with Portuguese subtitles (only children's films are dubbed). After dark, exercise caution in Cinelândia, where there's a large concentration of theaters.

In addition to its many museums, there are several privately funded cultural centers. These host changing, often exceptional art and photography exhibits as well as film series, lectures, and children's programs. All the big newspapers have daily cultural sections that tell what's going on in the city—in Portuguese.

Venues

ATL HALL (Av. Ayrton Senna 3000, Barra da Tijuca, tel. 021/3385–0516 for tickets, 021/2285–3773 for schedules) is a posh, 4,500-seat performance center in the Via Parque shopping complex. It hosts theater and dance performances, as well as shows by top-name performers.

CENTRO CULTURAL BANCO DO BRASIL (Rua 1° de Março 66, Centro, tel. 021/2216–0237, 021/2216–0626) was constructed in 1888 and was once the headquarters of the Bank of Brazil. In the late 1980s, this six-story domed building with marble floors was

Not a Night Owl?

You can learn a lot about a place if you take its pulse after dark. So even if you're the original early-to-bed type, there's every reason to vary your routine when you're away from home.

EXPERIENCE THE FAMILIAR IN A NEW PLACE *Whether your thing is going to the movies or going to concerts, it's always different away from home. In clubs, new faces and new sounds add up to a different scene. Or you may catch movies you'd never see at home.*

TRY SOMETHING NEW *Do something you've never done before. It's another way to dip into the local scene. A simple suggestion: Go out later than usual—go dancing late and finish up with breakfast at dawn.*

DO SOMETHING OFFBEAT *Look into lectures and readings as well as author appearances in book stores. You may even meet your favorite novelist.*

EXPLORE A DAYTIME NEIGHBORHOOD AT NIGHT *Take a nighttime walk through an explorable area you've already seen by day. You'll get a whole different view of it.*

ASK AROUND *If you strike up a conversation with like-minded people during the course of your day, ask them about their favorite spots. Your hotel concierge is another resource.*

DON'T WING IT *As soon as you've nailed down your travel dates, look into local publications or surf the Net to see what's on the calendar while you're in town. Look for hot regional acts, dance and theater, big-name performing artists, expositions, and sporting events. Then call or click to order tickets.*

CHECK OUT THE NEIGHBORHOOD *Whenever you don't know the neighborhood you'll be visiting, review safety issues with people in your hotel. What's the transportation situation? Can you walk there, or do you need a cab? Is there anything else you need to know?*

CASH OR CREDIT? *Know before you go. It's always fun to be surprised—but not when you can't cover your check.*

transformed into a cultural center for art exhibitions and music recitals. The complex features a library, two theaters, four video rooms, an auditorium, and a permanent display of Brazilian currency. Its gift shop is full of stunning coffee-table tomes on art and history—some in English. It's open Tuesday–Sunday 10–8.

FUNDAÇÃO CASA FRANÇA-BRASIL (Rua Visconde de Itaboraí 78, Centro, tel. 021/2253–5366) links France and Brazil in a cultural and artistic exchange. The interior of what was once a customs house has been completely restored, leaving an elegant, neoclassical space of gracious columns and arcades. Exhibits have included everything from photography and painting to displays on Carnaval and Brazil's environment. Musical shows (Gilberto Gil was a recent performer), poetry readings, and lectures round out the events. The center's hours are Tuesday–Sunday 10–8.

SALA CECÍLIA MEIRELES (Largo da Lapa 47, Centro, tel. 021/2232–4779) is a center for classical music.

TEATRO DULCINA (Rua Alcindo Guanabara 17, Centro, tel. 021/2240–4879), a 600-seat theater, features opera and classical concerts.

TEATRO JOÃO CAETANO (Praça Tiradentes, Centro, tel. 021/2221–0305) offers nightly variety shows—comedy, music, and dance—in a large theater setting.

TEATRO MUNICIPAL (Praça Floriano, Centro, tel. 021/2297–4411) is the city's main performing arts venue, hosting dance, opera (often with international divas as guest artists), symphony concerts, and theater events year-round—although the season officially runs from April to December. The theater also has its own ballet company, and is the site of an international ballet festival during April and May.

TEATRO PAÇO IMPERIAL (Praça 15 de Novembro 48, Centro, tel. 021/2533–4407), like the Teatro Municipal, features a varied schedule of theater, music, and dance performances.

In This Chapter

Updated by Ana Lúcia do Vale

where to stay

MOST OF RIO'S HOTELS are in Copacabana and Ipanema. Copacabana hotels are close to the action (and the metrô), but the neighborhood is noisier than Ipanema (which is itself noisier than São Conrado and Barra da Tijuca). Note that Rio's "motels" aren't aimed at tourists. They attract couples looking for privacy, and usually rent by the hour.

PRICES

In the days just prior to and during Carnaval, already peak-season rates can double, even triple. Expect to pay a premium for a room with a view. Many hotels include breakfast in the rate, but the quality varies from a full buffet to a hard roll with butter. Remember that if you're traveling during peak periods, make reservations as far in advance as possible. Air-conditioning is standard in most hotels, as are room safes. Room service is available in all $$$–$$$$ establishments; in $$–$$$$ hotels, you'll find concierges or, at the very least, reception personnel who perform concierge duties.

CATEGORY	COST*
$$$$	over R$400
$$$	R$300–R$400
$$	R$200–R$300
$	R$100–R$200
¢	under R$100

**for a double room in high season, excluding taxes*

$$$$ ★ CAESAR PARK. This beachfront hotel has established itself as a favorite of business travelers, celebrities, and heads of state, who appreciate its impeccable service. To assist business guests, the hotel provides secretarial services, as well as fax machines and laptops for in-room use. *Av. Vieira Souto 460, Ipanema 22120, tel. 021/2525–2525, 800/2223–6800 in the U.S, www.caesarpark-rio.com. 186 rooms, 32 suites. Restaurant, bar, pool, hair salon, massage, sauna, gym, baby-sitting, laundry service, business services, meeting room. AE, DC, MC, V.*

$$$$ ★ COPACABANA PALACE. Built in 1923 for the visiting king of Belgium, this was the first luxury hotel in South America. To this day, it retains more soul and elegance than any other hotel. It also served as the set for much of the 1933 Fred Astaire and Ginger Rogers film *Flying Down to Rio*. A face-lift restored its facade and left the individually decorated guest rooms with such luxurious touches as inlaid agate and mahogany; and computer, fax, and modem facilities. The Copa also has a rooftop tennis court and Rio's largest hotel pool. The Saturday feijoada is a social event extraordinaire, rivaling the gala Carnaval ball held here each year. *Av. Atlântica 1702, Copacabana 22021, tel. 021/2548–7070; 800/237–1236 in the U.S., fax 021/2235–7330, www.copacabanapalace.orient-express.com. 122 rooms, 102 suites. 2 restaurants, 2 bars, in-room data ports, pool, sauna, tennis court, health club, theater, business services, meeting room. AE, DC, MC, V. Metrô: Cardeal Arcoverde.*

$$$$ INTER-CONTINENTAL RIO. One of the city's few resorts is in São Conrado, on its own slice of beachfront next to the Gávea Golf and Country Club. Attractions include a cocktail lounge, a discotheque, a French restaurant (the Monseigneur), an Italian restaurant (the Alfredo), business facilities, and golf privileges. Every room has an original tapestry done by a Brazilian artist and a balcony overlooking the ocean. *Av. Prefeito Mendes de Morais 222, São Conrado 22600, tel. 021/3323–2200; 800/327–0200 in the U.S., fax 021/3323–5500, www.interconti.com. 391 rooms, 20 cabanas, 53 suites. 5 restaurants, 2 bars, piano bar, 3 pools, hair salon, sauna, golf privileges, 3 tennis courts, health club, shops, dance club, nightclub,* *business services, convention center, travel services, car rental.* AE, DC, MC, V.

$$$$ **SHERATON RIO HOTEL & TOWERS.** Built so that it dominates Vidigal, between Leblon and São Conrado, this is the only hotel in Rio with its own private beach (it's set on a bluff above the water and has a stairway down to the sand). Guest rooms are decorated in pastels, and all have beach views. The landscaping out by the pools is fabulous, and though the hotel isn't long on intimacy, the vistas are sublime. Be prepared for numerous taxi rides from this prime, though isolated, location. *Av. Niemeyer 121, Vidigal 22450, tel. 021/2274–1122; 800/325–3589 in the U.S., fax 021/2239–5643, www.sheraton-rio.com. 561 rooms, 22 suites. 4 restaurants, 2 bars, 3 pools, sauna, 3 tennis courts, gym, shops, nightclub, business services, meeting room, travel services, car rental.* AE, DC, MC, V. BP.

$$$$ **SOFITEL RIO PALACE.** Anchoring one end of Copacabana Beach, this hotel has been given a top-to-bottom face-lift and is, once again, one of the best on the strip. The building's H shape gives all rooms balcony views of the sea, the mountains, or both. One pool gets the morning sun; the other, afternoon rays. The rooftop bar areas are always lively. *Av. Atlântica 4240, Copacabana 22070, tel. 021/2525–1232; 800/7763–4835 in the U.S. 388 rooms, 12 suites. 2 restaurants, 2 bars, tea shop, 2 pools, sauna, health club, shops, nightclub, business services, convention center.* AE, DC, MC, V.

$$$–$$$$ **EXCELSIOR.** This hotel, part of the Windsor chain, may have been built in the 1950s, but its look is sleek and contemporary—from the sparkling marble lobby to the guest-room closets paneled in gleaming *jacarandá* (Brazilian redwood). Service is top rate. The expansive breakfast buffet—free for guests—is served in the hotel's window-banked restaurant facing the avenue and beach. The equally elaborate lunch and dinner buffets cost roughly R$25. The rooftop bar–pool area offers an escape from the hustle and bustle. Ask for a room with a water view. *Av. Atlântica 1800, Copacabana 22000, tel. 021/2257–1950; 800/444–UTELL in the U.S., fax 021/2257–1850, www.windsonrhoteis.com.br. 230 rooms. Restaurant,*

rio de janeiro lodging

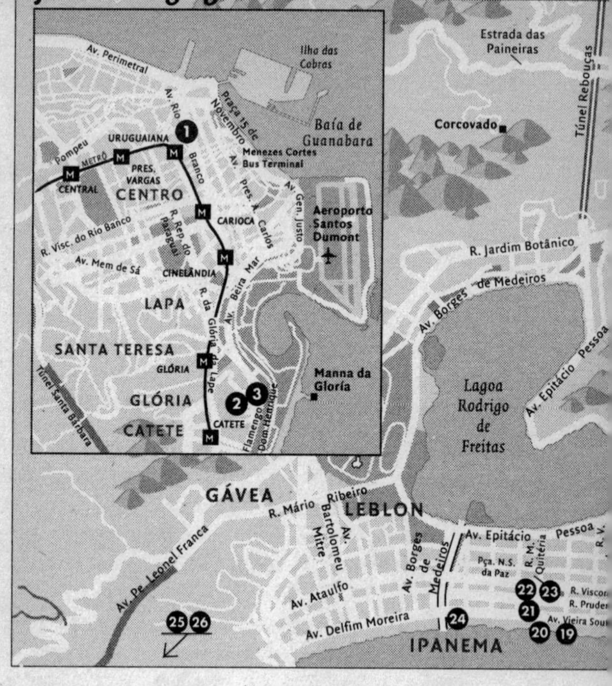

Arpoador Inn, 18
Atlântico Copacabana, 4
Caesar Park, 20
Copacabana Palace, 9
Debret, 15
Everest Rio, 22
Excelsior, 10
Glória, 2
Grandville Ouro Verde, 8
Guanabara Palace Hotel, 1
Inter-Continental Rio, 26
Ipanema Inn, 21
Leme Othon Palace, 6
Le Meridien, 7
Miramar Palace, 16
Novo Mundo, 3
Praia Ipanema, 24
Rio Atlântica, 13
Rio Internacional, 11
Rio Othon Palace, 14
Royalty Copacabana, 5
Sheraton Rio Hotel & Towers, 25

BOTAFOGO
Túnel Rebouças
BOTAFOGO
São Clemente
R. Voluntários da Pátria
Mena Barreto
R. General
R. Visconde de Silva
R. Real Grandeza
Av. das Nações Unidas
Av. Pasteur
A. Quintela
R. Alvaro Ramos Monteiro
Av. Princesa Isabel
CARDEAL AREOVERDE
TO CENTRO
Av. João Luis Alves
Av. São Sebastião
Sugarloaf
Av. Portugal
VERMELHA
N
R. Gustavo Sampaio
LEME
LAGOA
R. Tonelero
R. Baratas Ribeiro
Figueiredo Magalhães
R. Santa Clara
Copacabana
Av. Atlântica
OCEAN
COPACABANA
Parque da Catacumba
Av. Henrique Dodsworth
R. Raul Pompéia
Senhora de
Av. Nossa
ATLANTIC
R. V. de Morais
R. Farme de Amoedo
R. Visconde de Pirajá
R. Prudente de Morais
Vieira Souto
R. Gomes Carneiro
R. F. Otaviano
KEY
Cable Car
Metrô
0
1 mile
0
1 km

2 bars, pool, health club, meeting room. AE, DC, MC, V. BP. *Metrô: Cardeal Arcoverde.*

$$$–$$$$ LE MERIDIEN. Of the leading Copacabana hotels, the 37-story French-owned Meridien is the closest to Centro, making it a favorite of business travelers. Rooms are done in pastel tones with dark wood furniture. If you have work to do, the hotel has a complete executive center. Afterward, relax over a meal in Le Saint Honoré restaurant and then head for the jazz bar, which books some of the best acts in town. *Av. Atlântica 1020, Copacabana 22012, tel. 021/3873–8888, fax 021/3873–8777, www.meridien-br.com/rio. 443 rooms, 53 suites. 3 restaurants, bar, pool, hair salon, sauna, business services.* AE, DC, MC, V.

$$$ RIO OTHON PALACE. The flagship of the Brazilian Othon chain, this 30-story hotel is not new, but it does offer a prime view of Copacabana's distinctive black-and-white sidewalk mosaic from the rooftop pool, bar, and sundeck. The hotel has an executive floor, with secretarial support, fax machines, and computer hookups. *Av. Atlântica 3264, Copacabana 22070, tel. 021/2522–1522, fax 021/2522–1697, www.hoteis-othon.com.br. 554 rooms, 30 suites. 2 restaurants, 2 bars, pool, sauna, health club, nightclub, business services.* AE, DC, MC, V.

$$–$$$ EVEREST RIO. With standard service but one of Rio's finest rooftop views (a postcard shot of Corcovado and the lagoon), this hotel is in the heart of Ipanema's shopping and dining district, a block from the beach. Back rooms offer sea views. *Rua Prudente de Morais 1117, Ipanema 22420, tel. 021/2525–2200, fax 021/2521–3198, www.everest.com.br. 156 rooms, 11 suites. Restaurant, bar, pool, sauna, business services.* AE, DC, MC, V.

$$–$$$ MIRAMAR PALACE. The beachfront Miramar is a strange mix of old and new. Rooms are among the largest in Rio, and public areas are dominated by classic touches, from the Carrara marble floor of the lobby to the spectacular glass chandeliers that light the two restaurants. The hotel's 16th-floor bar is notable for its unobstructed view of the entire sweep of Copacabana; after 6 PM live Brazilian music adds a touch of romance. *Av. Atlântica 3668, Copacabana 22010, tel. 021/2521–1122, fax 021/2521–3294, www.hotelmiramar.com.br. 133 rooms, 11 suites. 2 restaurants, 2 bars, coffee shop, tearoom. AE, DC, MC, V. BP.*

$$–$$$ **PRAIA IPANEMA.** This hotel isn't deluxe, but it has a great location, and you can see the sea from all its rooms. Take in the dramatic beach view from the pool area on the roof of the 15-story building. You can also catch a breeze from your private balcony (every room has one). *Av. Vieira Souto 706, Ipanema 22420, tel. 021/2540–4949, fax 021/2239–6889, www.praiaipanema.com. 105 rooms. Bar, pool, beach. AE, DC, MC, V. BP.*

$$–$$$ **RIO ATLÂNTICA.** Though it's not luxurious, the Atlântica is well appointed and well maintained, offering rooftop sunbathing and swimming, a health club, and a bar with a view of Copacabana Beach. Although breakfast isn't included in the rates, standard rooms are (relatively) reasonably priced, and the service is superb. Business travelers will appreciate the meeting rooms and the secretarial support, which includes such services as simultaneous translation. *Av. Atlântica 2964, Copacabana 22070, tel. 021/2548–6332, fax 021/2255–6410. 108 rooms, 120 suites. Restaurant, 2 bars, pool, health club, business services, meeting room. AE, DC, MC, V.*

$$–$$$ **RIO INTERNACIONAL.** The red frame of this beachfront hotel has become a Copacabana landmark. Swiss owned and aimed at business travelers, the hotel offers a rarity for Avenida Atlântica: all rooms have balconies with sea views. All guests are welcomed with a glass of champagne. *Av. Atlântica 1500, Copacabana 22010, tel. 021/2543–1555, fax 021/2542–5443, www.riointernacional.com.br. 117 rooms, 12 suites. Restaurant, 2 bars, pool, sauna, business services. AE, DC, MC, V.*

$$ **LEME OTHON PALACE.** Large rooms and a quiet beachfront location have made this a hotel of choice with repeat visitors. Built in 1964, it has a subdued, conservative air, lacking a few of the most modern amenities. *Av. Atlântica 656, Leme 22010, tel. 021/2543–8080 or 021/2546–1010, www.hoteis-othon.com.br. 168 rooms, 26 suites. Restaurant, bar.* AE, DC, MC, V.

$$ SOL IPANEMA. Another of Rio's crop of tall, slender hotels, this one has a great location, anchoring the eastern end of Ipanema Beach. All rooms have motel-style beige carpets and drapes and light-color furniture; deluxe front rooms have panoramic beach views, while back rooms from the eighth floor up, which are the same size, have views of the lagoon and Corcovado. *Av. Vieira Souto 320, Ipanema 22420, tel. 021/2525–2028, fax 021/2247–8484, www.solipanema.com.br. 66 rooms, 12 suites. Restaurant, bar, pool.* AE, DC, MC, V. BP.

$–$$ GRANDVILLE OURO VERDE. For three decades, folks have favored this hotel for its efficient, personalized service. The tasteful Brazilian colonial decor and dark-wood furniture are in step with the emphasis on quality and graciousness. All front rooms face the beach; those in the back on the 6th to 12th floors have a view of Corcovado. *Av. Atlântica 1456, Copacabana 22041, tel. 021/2543–4123, fax 021/2542–4597, www.grandville.com.br. 61 rooms, 5 suites. Restaurant, bar, library.* AE, DC, MC, V.

$–$$ GUANABARA PALACE HOTEL. Another member of the Windsor chain, the recently renovated Guanabara is one of the only solid hotel choices right in Centro. Rooms are reasonably sized and tastefully done in brown and beige. Like the one in its sister hotel, the Excelsior, the restaurant serves elaborate buffet meals, and breakfast is included in the rate. The contemporary rooftop pool area, with its stunning views of Guanabara Bay, absolutely gleams thanks to its pristine white tiles, white trellises, and white patio furnishings. *Av. Presidente Vargas 392, Centro 22071, tel. 021/2518–0333, fax 021/2516–1582, www.windsorhoteis.com.br. 326 rooms. Restaurant, bar, minibars, room service, pool, sauna, health club, business services, meeting room, parking (fee).* AE, DC, MC, V. BP. *Metrô: Uruguaiana.*

$ ARPOADOR INN. This pocket-size hotel occupies the stretch of sand known as Arpoador. Surfers ride the waves, and pedestrians rule the roadway—a traffic-free street allows direct beach access. The hotel is simple but comfortable. At sunset the view from the rocks that mark the end of the beach is considered one of Rio's most beautiful. The spectacle is visible from the hotel's back rooms; avoid the front rooms, which are on the noisy side. *Rua Francisco Otaviano 177, Ipanema 22080, tel. 021/2523–6092, fax 021/2511–5094, www.ipanema.com/hotel/arpoador_inn.htm. 46 rooms, 2 suites. Restaurant, bar. AE, DC, MC, V. BP.*

$ **ATLÂNTICO COPACABANA.** The large lobby may look modern to some, pretentious to others. Guest rooms are slightly larger than average. Although the Atlântico is in a noisy residential area, it's only four blocks from the beach. *Rua Sigueira Campos 90, Copacabana 20000, tel. 021/2548–0011, fax 021/2235–7941, www.atlanticocopacabana.com.br. 97 rooms, 18 suites. Restaurant, 3 bars, pool, hair salon, sauna. AE, DC, MC, V. BP. Metrô: Cardeal Arcoverde.*

$ **DEBRET.** This former apartment building scores points for keeping its prices moderate despite a beachfront location. The decor honors Brazil's past: the lobby has baroque statues and prints depicting colonial scenes, and the rooms are furnished in dark, heavy wood. The hotel has a loyal following among diplomats and businesspeople who are more interested in functionality and low prices than elegance. *Av. Atlântica 3564, Copacabana 22041, tel. 021/2522–0132, fax 021/2521–0899, www.debret.com. 90 rooms, 10 suites. Restaurant, bar. AE, DC, MC, V. BP.*

$ **GLÓRIA.** A grande dame of Rio's hotels, this classic was built in 1922 and is full of French antiques. What makes it a draw for business travelers (it's a five-minute cab ride from Centro) may discourage sun worshipers (it's a slightly longer cab ride from the beaches). *Rua do Russel 632, Glória 22210, tel. 021/2205–7272, fax 021/2555–7282, www.hotelgloriario.com.br. 596 rooms, 20 suites. 4 restaurants, 3 bars, 2 pools, sauna, gym, meeting room. AE, DC, MC, V. BP. Metrô: Glória.*

$ **IPANEMA INN.** This small, no-frills hotel was built for those who want to stay in Ipanema but have no interest in paying the high prices of beachfront accommodations. Just a half block from the beach, it's convenient not only for sun worshipers but also for those seeking to explore Ipanema's varied nightlife. *Rua Maria Quitéria 27, Ipanema 22410, tel. 021/2523–6092 or 021/2274–6995. 56 rooms. Bar, dining room. AE, DC, MC, V. BP.*

$ **ROYALTY COPACABANA.** Set three blocks from the beach, this hotel is convenient for beachgoers yet removed enough to satisfy those looking for peace and quiet. Moderate prices are a plus. The back rooms from the third floor up are the quietest and have mountain views; front rooms face the sea. *Rua Tonelero 154, Copacabana 22030, tel. 021/2548–5699, fax 021/2255–1999. 130 rooms, 13 suites. Restaurant, bar, pool, sauna, gym. AE, DC, MC, V. BP. Metrô: Cardeal Arcoverde.*

$ **TOLEDO.** Although it has few amenities, the Toledo goes the extra mile to make the best of what it does have. The staff is friendly, the service is efficient, and the location—on a quiet back street of Copacabana, a block from the beach—isn't bad either. Back rooms from the 9th to the 14th floors have sea views and sliding floor-to-ceiling windows. *Rua Domingos Ferreira 71, Copacabana 22050, tel. 021/2257–1990, fax 021/2287–7640. 87 rooms, 8 suites. Bar, coffee shop. DC, MC, V. BP.*

$ **VERMONT.** This hotel is clean, reliable, and just two blocks from the beach—a good choice for budget travelers. Its only drawback is its location on the main street of Ipanema, which means incessant noise during the day (it tends to quiet down after the shops close). *Rua Visconde de Pirajá 254, Ipanema 22410, tel. 021/2522–0057, fax 021/2267–7046. 54 rooms. Bar, dining room. AE, DC, MC, V. BP.*

¢–$ **NOVO MUNDO.** A short walk from the Catete metrô station, this traditional hotel sits astride Guanabara Bay in Flamengo, near Glória. Convention rooms are popular with the business crowd, and there is a parking garage with daily or hourly rates. All rooms have air-conditioning, closet with safe, TV with cable channels in English, a small refrigerator, and a writing desk. Deluxe rooms have a view of the bay. *Praia do Flamengo 20, Flamengo 22210–030, tel. 021/2557–6226 or 0800/225–3355. 217 rooms, 10 suites. Restaurant, bar, hair salon. AE, D, MC, V. BP. Metrô: Catete.*

In This Chapter

Updated by Ana Lúcia do Vale

side trips

RIO THE STATE HAS JUST AS MUCH ALLURE as Rio the city. Across Guanabara Bay, Niterói is a mix of new and old: the ultramodern Museu de Arte Contemporânea is set not too far from historic forts. A scenic northeast road into the mountains leads to Petrópolis, a city that bears testimony to the country's royal legacy. Beyond, tucked into a lush valley, is charming Nova Friburgo with its Swiss ambience. Due east of the city, dangling off the yacht-frequented coast, are the sophisticated resort towns of Cabo Frio and Búzios, where Rio's chic escape for weekends. And to the southwest along the Costa Verde sit the stunning Angra dos Reis—facing the offshore island of Ilha Grande—and the colonial city of Parati, with its 18th century Portuguese architecture and plethora of offshore islets.

NITERÓI

14 km (9 mi) *east of* Rio.

Ranked as having the highest quality of life in Rio de Janeiro state, Niterói, literally, "hidden waters," was founded in 1573. Old and new come together in this city of 453,000, where both a modern naval industry and traditional fishing help support the economy. Ocean beaches and the Fortaleza de Santa Cruz—an ancient fortress built in 1555 to protect the bay—draw visitors, but so does the ultramodern Museu de Arte Contemporânea. Ferries from Riio's Praça 15 de Novembro cross the bay, arriving at Praça Araribóia in a pleasant 20 minutes.

The must-see **MUSEU DE ARTE CONTEMPORÂNEA** was constructed by the well-known architect Oscar Niemeyer (he designed most of Brazil's capital—Brasília). Opened in September 1996, the building looks a bit like a spaceship. The modern art museum shelters the collection donated by João Sattamini. Just five minutes from Praça Araribóia (in downtown Niterói where the ferries stop), enjoy a nice walk along the coastline. Upon leaving, try the fresh coconut water sold outside. *Estrada de Boa Viagem, Boa Viagem, tel. 021/2620–2400. R$2. Tues.–Fri. 11–7, Sat. 1–9, Sun 11–7.*

The **FORTALEZA DE SANTA CRUZ** was the first fort built on Guanabara Bay, in 1555. Distributed on two floors are cannons, a sun clock, and the Santa Barbara Chapel—dating from the 17th century. It's best to visit in the cool morning hours. Fifteen minutes from downtown, it's an easy taxi ride (R$15), or there's a bus that goes straight to Jurujuba (No. 33) from the ferry dock. *Estrada General Eurico Gaspar Dutra, Jurujuba, tel. 021/2711–0462. R$3. Daily 9–5.*

Built as an lookout point, **FORTE BARÃO DO RIO BRANCO** was armed and turned into a battery in 1567. Inside is the Forte do Imbuí, another fortress, which is a wonderful place to walk, with a great view of Guanabara Bay and Rio. *Av. Marechal Pessoa Leal 265, Jurujuba, tel. 021/2711–0366 or 021/2711–0566. R$3. Weekends, holidays 9–5.*

PETRÓPOLIS

65 km (42 mi) northeast of Rio.

The hilly highway northeast of the city rumbles past forests and waterfalls en route to a mountain town so refreshing and picturesque that Dom Pedro II, Brazil's second emperor, spent his summers in it. (From 1889 to 1899, it was also the country's year-round seat of government.) Horse-drawn carriages shuttle between the sights, passing flowering gardens, shady parks, and imposing pink mansions.

rio de janeiro state

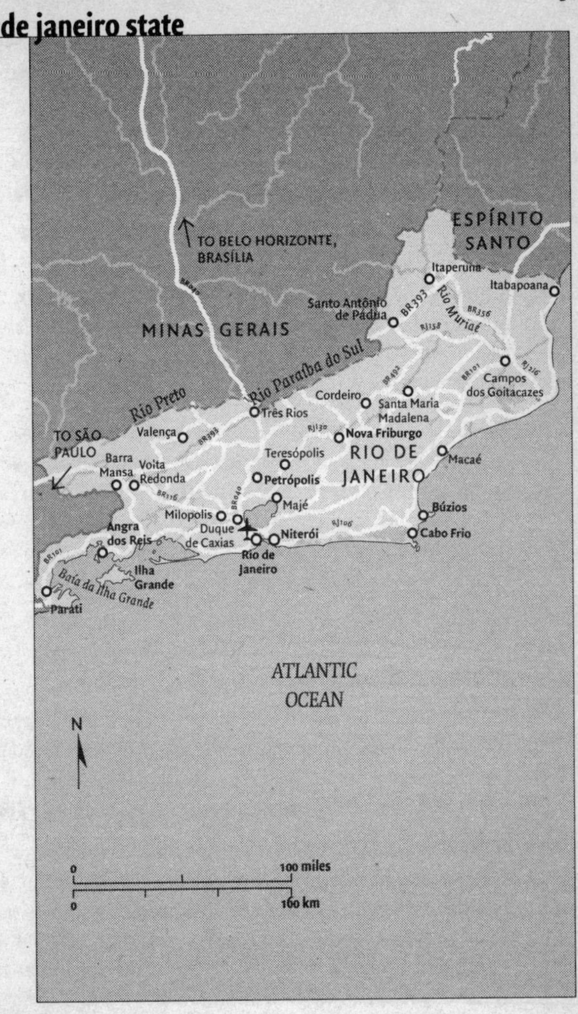

The **MUSEU IMPERIAL** is a museum housed in the magnificent 44-room palace that was Dom Pedro's summer home, the colossal structure is filled with polished wooden floors, 19th-century artwork, and grand chandeliers. You can also see the diamond-encrusted gold crown and scepter of Brazil's last emperor, as well as other royal jewels. *Rua da Imperatriz 220, tel. 024/2237–8000. R$4. Tues.–Sun. noon–5:30.*

From the Museu Imperial, you can walk three long blocks or take a horse-drawn carriage to **SÃO PEDRO DE ALCANTARA**, the Gothic cathedral containing the tombs of Dom Pedro II; his wife, Dona Teresa Cristina; and their daughter, Princesa Isabel. *Av. Tiradentes, no phone. Free. Weekdays 8–noon, Sun. 8–6.*

The **PALÁCIO DE CRISTAL** (Crystal Palace), a stained-glass and iron building made in France and assembled in Brazil, was a wedding present to Princesa Isabel. During the imperial years it was used as a ballroom: it was here the princess held a celebration dance after she abolished slavery in Brazil in 1888. *Praça da Confluencia, Rua Alfredo Pacha, no phone. Free. Tues.–Sun. 9–5.*

Dining and Lodging

$–$$ **BAUERNSTUBE.** German food is the backbone of this log cabin–style eatery. The bratwurst and sauerkraut are properly seasoned, and the strudel is an excellent choice for polishing off a meal. *Dr. Nelson de Sá Earp 297, tel. 024/2442–1097. AE, DC, MC, V. Closed Mon.*

$–$$$ **POUSADA DE ALCOBAÇA.** Just north of Petrópolis, this is considered by many to be the loveliest inn in the area. The grounds have beautiful gardens and a swimming pool. The kitchen turns out exceptional breakfasts, lunches, and high teas with an emphasis on fresh ingredients. Meals, which include savory pastas, are served in the garden. *Agostinho Goulao 298, Correa, tel. 024/2221–1240, fax 024/2222–3390. 10 rooms. Restaurant, pool, sauna, tennis court. AE, DC, MC, V. BP.*

$–$$$ **POUSADA MONTE IMPERIAL.** A few minutes from downtown, this Euro-style inn has 14 double rooms with private baths, a pool, a lobby with a fireplace, and a restaurant-bar. Drinks and meals can also be taken in the lovely garden. *Rua Joséde Alencar 27, tel. 024/2237–1664. 14 rooms. Restaurant, bar, pool. AE, DC, MC, V. BP.*

¢ **HOTEL MARGARIDAS.** Three chalets and 12 apartments make up this comfortable complex just five minutes from the heart of downtown. You'll find well-tended gardens and a swimming pool. *Rua Bispo Pereira Alves 235, tel. 024/2442–4686. 12 apartments, 3 chalets. Pool. AE, DC, MC, V. BP.*

NOVA FRIBURGO

131 km (79 mi) northeast of Petrópolis; 196 km (121 mi) northeast of Rio.

This summer resort town was settled by Swiss immigrants in the early 1800s, when Brazil was actively encouraging European immigration and when the economic situation in Switzerland was bad. Woods, rivers, and waterfalls dot the terrain encircling the city. Homemade liquors, jams, and cheeses pack the shelves of the town's small markets. Cariocas come here to unwind in the cool mountain climate.

A cable car rises more than 600 m (2,000 ft) to **MORRO DA CRUZ,** which offers a spectacular view of the mountain. *Praça Teleférica, no phone. Admission R$10. Weekends 9–6.*

Lodging

$ **HOTEL BUCSKY.** Long walks through the several thousand kilometers of forests that surrounds the hotel are among the draws at this country-house inn. Meals are included, and if the restaurant is not luxurious, it does serve honest food, self-service style. *Estrada Rio-Friburgo, Km 76.5, Ponte Saudade 28615-160, tel. 024/2522–5052 or 024/2522–5500, fax 024/2522–9769. 60 rooms, 10 suites. Pool, sauna, miniature golf, tennis court. AE, DC, MC, V. FAP.*

CABO FRIO

168 km (101 mi) east of Rio.

Set up as a defensive port from which to ship wood to Portugal nearly four centuries ago, Cabo Frio has evolved into a resort town renowned for its fresh seafood. It's also a prime jumping-off point for the endless number of white-sand beaches that crisscross the area around town and the offshore islands. A favorite sailing destination, its turquoise waters are crowded with sailboats and yachts on holidays and weekends. The town itself has attractive baroque architecture.

Praia do Forte is popular thanks to its calm, clear waters and long stretch of sand. On weekends it's jammed with colorful beach umbrellas, swimmers, and sun lovers. Some distance away, Praia Brava and Praia do Foguete lure surfers to their crashing waves.

BÚZIOS

★ *25 km (15 mi) northeast of Cabo Frio; 193 km (126 mi) northeast of* Rio.

Búzios, a little more than two hours from Rio, is a string of gorgeous beaches that draws resort fans year-round from Europe and South America. This is the perfect place to do absolutely nothing. It was little more than a fishing village until the 1960s, when Brigitte Bardot was photographed here in a bikini. Since then, Búzios's rustic charm has given way to *pousadas*, or inns (some of them luxurious, few inexpensive); restaurants; and bars run by people who came on vacation and never left. The balance between the cosmopolitan and the primitive is seductive.

March through June is low season, when temperatures range from about 27°C (80°F) to 32°C (90°F), and prices often drop 30%–40%. The water is still warm, yet the crowds aren't as great; the area seems much more intimate than in the summer months of October through December. Though not a great deal of English is spoken here, a little Spanish or French will get you a long way.

Each of the beaches offers something different: the lovely, intimate Azeda and Azedinha are local favorites (and the spots where you may find topless bathing); Ferradura is known for the gastronomic excellence of its kiosks and its jet skiing; Lagoinha is referred to by all as a magic beach and has a natural amphitheater where world-class musicians hold concerts; Brava is the surfers' beach; and Manguinhos is popular with windsurfers.

Dining and Lodging

$$$–$$$$ ★ **SATYRICON.** The Italian fish restaurant famous in Rio has opened up shop here as well. The menu's highlight is the expensive but great seafood, including the restaurant's famous rock salt–baked whole fish, which music star Madonna has tried and approved. *Av. José Bento Ribeiro Dantas 412, tel. 024/2223–1595. AE, DC, MC, V.*

$$–$$$$ ★ **CIGALON.** The restaurant has a veranda overlooking the beach. It's the only place that serves lamb steak for R$27. The cooked lobster with rice and almonds for R$42 is a must-eat. If you're having trouble making up your mind among the tempting options, the tasting menu for R$33 might be your best bet. *Rua das Pedras 151, tel. 024/2223–6284. AE, DC, MC, V.*

$ **CHEZ MICHOU.** This *crêperie* on the main drag in the center of town is the best place to eat if you want something quick, light, and inexpensive. You can choose from about 500 different crepe fillings and then eat your meal outdoors. At night locals and visitors alike congregate to drink and people-watch. *Rua José Bento Ribeiro Dantas 90, tel. 024/2223–6137. No credit cards.*

$$–$$$ ★ **BARRACUDA.** This hotel is included in Brazil's esteemed Roteiros de Charme club, a highly exclusive association of the nation's best places to stay. The view of the sea from the deck is breathtaking. *Ponta da Sapata, tel. 021/2287–3122, Ext. 601 for reservations from Rio,*

tel./fax 024/2223–1314. 23 rooms. Restaurant, pool, sauna, 2 tennis courts. AE, DC, MC, V. BP.

ANGRA DOS REIS

151 km (91 mi) west of Rio.

Angra dos Reis, the Bay of Kings, anchors the rugged Costa Verde in an area of beautiful beaches, colonial architecture, and clear emerald waters. Schooners, yachts, sailboats, and fishing skiffs thread among the 365 offshore islands, one for every day of the year. Indeed, Angra dos Reis's popularity lies in its strategic location—ideal for exploring those islands, many of which are deserted patches of sand and green that offer wonderful swimming and snorkeling opportunities. Organized boat tours from shore can take you to favored island haunts.

One of the most popular islands is the lush, mountainous **ILHA GRANDE.** Just 2 km (1 mi), a 90-minute ferry ride off the shore from Angra dos Reis, it has more than 100 idyllic beaches—sandy ribbons that stretch on and on with a backdrop of tropical foliage. The boats arrive at Vila do Abraão. From there you can roam paths that lead from one slip of sand to the next or negotiate with local boatmen for jaunts to the beaches or more remote islets.

A 10-minute walk takes you to the hot waters off the beaches Praia da Júlia and Comprida. After a 25-minute walk is the transparent sea at Abraãozinho Beach. If you choose to go by boat, don't miss the big waves of Lopes Mendes Beach or the astonishing blue, Mediterraneanlike water of Lagoa Azul. Scuba diving fans should head to Gruta do Acaiá to see turtles and other colorful South American fish.

Dining and Lodging

$$$–$$$$ **HOTEL DO FRADE & GOLF RESORT.** Guest-room balconies overlook the sea and a private beach at this modern resort hotel.

For those who love sports, the property offers many options: an 18-hole golf course, seven tennis courts, a soccer field, and, of course, jet skis and other boat rentals. The hotel can also arrange excursions on the Ilha Grande Bay or scuba diving. It's no surprise that seafood is good at the buffet restaurant Scuna. In the summer, other resort restaurants offer a variety of international cuisines. *BR 101, Km 123, Praia do Frade, tel. 024/3369–9500, fax 024/3369–2254. 160 rooms. 3 restaurants, bar, swimming pool, tennis courts, 18-hole golf, soccer, jet skiing, boating, cinema, baby-sitting.* AE, D, DC, MC, V. FAP.

$$–$$$$ **PARAÍSO DOS REIS.** Opened in 2000, this comfortable hotel has a private beach. Electric cars shuttle guests from the door of their chalets to the sand. Water activities abound, including jet ski and boat rental. *Estrada do Contorno 3700, Retiro, tel. 024/3367–2654, fax 024/3367–2654. 30 rooms. Bar, pool, massage, sauna, jet skiing, boating.* AE, D, DC, MC, V.

$–$$ **PORTOGALO SUÍTE.** Perched on the top of a hill with a wonderful view of the bay, the exposed-brick buildings have a rustic appeal. The rooms are cozy and comfy and a cable car is available to take guests down the hillside to the beach and the marina. BR 101, Km 71, *Praia de Itapinhoacanga, tel. 024/3361–4343, fax 024/3361–4361. 70 rooms. Bar, pool, sauna, 2 tennis courts, jet skiing.* AE, D, DC, MC, V.

PARATI

100 km (60 mi) southwest of Angra dos Reis.

This stunning colonial city is one of South America's gems. Giant iron chains hang from posts at the beginning of the mazelike grid of cobblestone streets, closing them to all but pedestrians, horses, and bicycles. Until the 18th century, this was an important transit point for gold plucked from the Minas Gerais—a safe harbor protected from pirates by a fort. (The cobblestones are the rock ballast brought from Lisbon, then unloaded to make room in the ships for their golden cargoes.) In 1720, however, the colonial powers cut a new trail from the gold mines straight to Rio de Janeiro, bypassing the town and leaving it isolated. It remained that way until contemporary times, when artists, writers, and others "discovered" the community and UNESCO placed it on its World Heritage Site list. Brazilian actress Sonia Braga comes here to relax, and Rolling Stone Mick Jagger used it as the backdrop for a music video.

Parati isn't a city peppered with lavish mansions and opulent palaces; rather it has a simple beauty. By the time the sun breaks over the bay each morning—illuminating the whitewashed, colorfully trimmed buildings—the fishermen will have begun spreading out their catch at the outdoor market. The best way to explore is simply to begin walking winding streets banked with centuries-old buildings that hide quaint inns, tony restaurants, shops, and art galleries. Once you've finished your in-town exploration, you can begin investigating what makes this a weekend escape for cariocas: the lush, tropical offshore islands and not-so-distant strands of coastal beach.

Parati is jammed with churches, but the most intriguing are the trio whose congregations were segregated by race during the colonial era. **IGREJA DE NOSSA SENHORA DO ROSÁRIO** (Rua do Comércio) was built by the town's slaves so they could have their own place of worship. Simple and clean-lined **IGREJA DE SANTA RITA** (Rua Santa Rita), meanwhile, was built in 1722 and earmarked for free mulattoes; today it houses a small religious art museum. On the far extreme of the social spectrum, **IGREJA DE NOSSA SENHORA DAS DORES** (Rua Dr. Pereira) was the church of the community's small but elite white population. The fortress, **FORTE DEFENSOR PERPÉTUO** (Morro da Vila Velha), was built in the early 1700s (and rebuilt in 1822) as a defense against pirates and is now home to a folk-arts center. It sits north of town.

Dining and Lodging

$–$$ **AMIGO DO REI.** You can find typical food from the Brazilian countryside, as well as seafood, at this cozy, quiet spot. It's one of the best eateries in town—both because of the kitchen and because of the prices. *Rua Dona Geralda 174, Centro Histórico de Parati, tel. 024/3371–1049. No credit cards. No lunch.*

$ ★ **PORTO POUSADA PARATI.** Rooms in this historic structure in the oldest part of town ring a series of courtyards and a swimming pool. Rates include breakfast. *Rua do Comércio, tel. 024/3371–1205, fax 024/3371–2111. 51 rooms. Restaurant, bar, pool, sauna. AE, DC, MC, V.*

¢–$ **POUSADA DO OURO.** Inside an 18th-century building with a garden courtyard, this is the inn most likely to host celebrities who come to the area for sun and atmosphere. *Rua da Praia 145, tel. 024/3371–1378, fax 024/3371–1311. 18 rooms, 8 suites Restaurant, bar, pool. AE, DC, MC, V. BP.*

¢ ★ **POUSADA DO PRÍNCIPE.** A prince (the great grandson of Emperor Pedro II) owns this aptly named inn at the edge of the colonial city. The hotel is painted in the yellow and green of the imperial flag, and its quiet, colorful public areas are graced by photos of the royal family. Rooms are small but comfortable (and air-conditioned). The swimming pool in the plant-filled patio beckons. The kitchen is impressive, too; its chef turns out an exceptional feijoada. *Av. Roberto Silveira 289, tel. 024/3371–2266, fax 024/3371–2120. 34 rooms. Restaurant, pool, sauna, 2 tennis courts. AE, DC, MC, V.*

SIDE TRIPS FROM RIO A TO Z

Boat and Ferry Travel

To get to Niterói, there are ferries available at Praça 15 de Novembro in Rio. In 20 minutes you'll arrive at Praça Araribóia, in downtown Niterói. There is no car service available. Barcas boats are bigger and slower than the newer Catamaran Jumbo Cat fleet.

To get to Ilha Grande, Vila do Abraão, you have two options run by Barcas. A ferry leaves Angra dos Reis, from Cais da Lapa at Avenida dos Reis Magos, daily at 3:15 PM. The return ferry departs weekdays at 10 AM and weekends at 11 AM. Or depart from Mangaratiba, at Avenida Mangaratiba, weekdays at 8 AM and weekends at 9AM. The ferry back from Vila do Abraão to Mangaratiba leaves daily at 5:30 PM. Either trip takes an hour and a half.

➤ **BOAT AND FERRY INFORMATION: Barcas S/A** (Praça Araribóia 6–8, Niterói, tel. 021/2719–1892 or 021/2620–6766; tel. Ilha Grande information: 021/2533–6661). **Catamaran Jumbo Cat** (Praça Araribóia s/n, Niterói, tel. 021/2620–8589 or 021/2620–8670).

Bus Travel

Several bus companies, including 1001, depart for Niterói from the Menezes Cortes Terminal (downtown Rio); from Avenida Princesa Isabel in Copacabana; and from Botafogo at the beach.

Leaving hourly from Rio's Rodoviária Novo Rio, Costa Verde buses travel to Petrópolis, Única buses to Angra dos Reis, and 12 buses a day head for Parati. Regional bus services connect Petrópolis with Nova Friburgo and Parati with Angra dos Reis.

Buses, a shuttle service, and airplanes regularly travel to and from popular Búzios and Rio. The best option is the shuttle service, which will pick you up in Rio in the morning and drop you at your pousada before noon. Contact Turismo Clássico Travel in Rio for reservations. Municipal buses connect Cabo Frio and Búzios.

➤ **BUS INFORMATION: Costa Verde** (tel. 021/2573–1484). **1001** (tel. 021/2613–1001 or 021/3849–5001). **Única** (tel. 021/2263–8792).

Car Travel

To reach Niterói by car, take the 14-km-long (9-mi-long) Presidente Costa e Silva Bridge, also known as Rio-Niterói. BR 101 connects the city to the Costa Verde and Parati. You'll need to head north and along BR 040 to reach the mountain towns of Petrópolis and Novo Friburgo. Coastal communities Cabo Frio and Búzios are east of Rio along or off RJ 106.

Money Matters

There are banks and ATMs in each community, but it's best to get reais before leaving Rio. Check in advance with your hotel to make sure credit cards are accepted.

Transportation Around Outlying Areas of Rio

You can rent cars, dune buggies, motorcycles, and bicycles at most of these destinations—or you can simply take taxis around each area. Ask the staff at your hotel or at the tourist offices for recommendations.

Visitor Information

Tourist offices are generally open weekdays from 8 or 8:30 to 6 and Saturday from 8 or 9 to 4; some have limited Sunday hours, too. The Niterói Tourism Office is open daily 9 to 6.

➤ **TOURIST INFORMATION: Angra dos Reis Tourism Office** (across from bus station on Rua Largo da Lapa, tel. 024/3365–1175, Ext. 2186). **Búzios Tourism Office** (Praça Santos Dumont 111, tel. 024/2623–2099). **Cabo Frio Tourism Office** (Av. de Contorno, Praia do Forte, tel. 024/2647–1689). **Niterói Tourism Office** (Estrada Leopoldo Fróes 773, São Francisco, tel. 021/2710–2727). **Nova Friburgo Tourism Office** (Praça Dr. Demervel B. Moreira, tel. 024/2523–8000). **Parati Tourism Office** (Av. Roberto Silveira, tel. 024/3371–1266, Ext. 217). **Petrópolis Tourism Office** (Praça da Confluencia 3, tel. 024/2243–3561).

practical information

Addresses

In Portuguese *avenida* (avenue) and *travessa* (lane) are abbreviated (as *Av.* and *Trv.* or *Tr.*), while other common terms such as *estrada* (highway) and *rua* (street) often aren't. Street numbers follow the names; postal codes are widely used. In some places street numbering doesn't enjoy the wide popularity it has achieved elsewhere; hence, you may find the notation "s/n," meaning "no street number."

Air Travel

Atlanta, Chicago, Houston, Los Angeles, Miami, Newark, New York, and Toronto are the major gateways for flights to Brazil from the United States and Canada. Several airlines fly directly from London, but there's no direct service from Australia or New Zealand.

Ponte Aérea (Air Bridge), the Rio–São Paulo shuttle departs every half hour from 6 AM to 10:30 PM (service switches to every 15 minutes during morning and evening rush hours). Plane tickets (one-way) for the Rio–São Paulo shuttle service cost R$50–R$190 ($23–$88); reservations aren't necessary.

AIRPORTS & TRANSFERS

All international flights and most domestic flights arrive and depart from the Aeroporto Internacional Antônio Carlos Jobim, also known as Galeão. The airport is about 45 minutes northwest of the beach area and most of Rio's hotels. Aeroporto Santos

Dumont, 20 minutes from the beaches and within walking distance of Centro, serves the Rio–São Paulo air shuttle and a few air-taxi firms.

Special airport taxis have booths in the arrival areas of both airports. Fares to all parts of Rio are posted at the booths, and you pay in advance (about R$35–R$50). Also trustworthy are the white radio taxis parked in the same areas; these charge an average of 20% less. Three reliable special-taxi firms are Transcoopass, Cootramo, and Coopertramo. **Write your destination down on a piece of paper** and present it to bus or taxi drivers, most of whom don't speak English.

Air-conditioned *frescão* buses run by Empresa Real park curbside outside customs at Galeão and outside the main door at Santos Dumont; for less than R$7 they make the hour-long trip from the former into the city, following the beachfront drives and stopping at all hotels along the way. If your hotel is inland, the driver will let you off at the nearest corner. Buses leave from the airport every half hour from 5:20 AM to 11 PM.

➤ **AIRPORT INFORMATION: Aeroporto Internacional Antônio Carlos Jobim** (tel. 021/3398–4526 or 0800/99–9099). **Aeroporto Santos Dumont** (tel. 021/2524–7070 or 0800/224–4646).

➤ **TAXIS AND SHUTTLES: Cootramo** (tel. 021/2560–5442). **Coopertramo** (tel. 021/2560–2022). **Empresa Real** (tel. 021/2290–5665 or 021/2270–7041). **Transcoopass** (tel. 021/2560–4888).

CARRIERS

Nearly three dozen airlines regularly serve Rio. International carriers include: American Airlines, British Airways, Canadian Airlines, Delta, and United. Several domestic carriers serve international and Brazilian destinations: Transbrasil, Varig, and VASP. Nordeste/RioSul covers domestic routes.

From London's Heathrow Airport you can take American or United and fly to Brazil via Miami or New York. Varig has nonstop flights from Heathrow to São Paulo with continuing service to Rio. British Airways has nonstop service from both Heathrow and Gatwick Airports to Rio. Continental flies from Gatwick and Heathrow to Newark and Houston with connecting flights to Rio.

From Sydney, Australia, you can fly to Los Angeles, then continue to Brazil on Varig. Another option is to fly Qantas to Buenos Aires, Argentina, where you connect to either Varig or Transbrasil. Air New Zealand offers flights to major Brazilian cities through its partnership with Varig. Direct flights to Los Angeles—where you transfer to Varig—depart from Auckland once or twice a day.

TAM, Transbrasil, and Varig are Brazil-based international carriers. TAM, which has an agreement with American Airlines that allows passengers to accumulate AA miles and awards, flies nonstop from Miami to São Paulo, with continuing service to Rio and connections to other cities. Transbrasil offers daily service from Orlando via Miami from which it continues nonstop to São Paulo. From there, you can catch connecting flights on Transbrasil to virtually all major Brazilian cities.

Varig, Latin America's largest carrier, has service to Rio from Los Angeles, Miami, and New York.

➤ **BRAZILIAN CARRIERS: TAM** (tel. 888/235–9826 in the U.S.; 305/406–2826 in Miami). **Transbrasil** (tel. 800/872–3153 in the U.S.). **Varig** (tel. 800/468–2744 in the U.S.). **VASP** (tel. 021/3814–8079, 021/2292–2112, 021/2462–3363, or 0800/99–8277).

➤ **NORTH AMERICAN CARRIERS: Air Canada** (tel. 888/247–2262 in North America). **American Airlines** (tel. 800/433–7300 in North America). **Continental Airlines** (tel. 800/231–0856 in North America). **Delta Airlines** (tel. 800/241–4141 in North America). **United Airlines** (tel. 800/241–6522 in North America).

➤ **FROM AUSTRALIA AND NEW ZEALAND: Air New Zealand** (tel. 13–24–76 in Australia; 0800/737–000 in New Zealand). **Qantas** (tel. 13–13–13 in Australia; 357–8900 in Auckland; 0800/808–767 rest of New Zealand).

➤ **FROM THE U.K.: American Airlines** (tel. 0845/778–9789). **British Airways** (tel. 0845/773–3377). **Continental Airlines** (tel. 0800/776–464). **TAM Airlines** (tel. 0207/707–4586. **United Airlines** (tel. 0845/844–4777). **Varig** (tel. 0207/478–2114).

CHECK-IN & BOARDING

Always **bring a government-issued photo ID to the airport.** You may be asked to show it before you're allowed to check in. **Be prepared to show your passport when leaving Brazil and to pay a hefty departure tax**, which runs about R$78 ($36) for international flights. A departure tax also applies to flights within Brazil. Although the amount varies, figure on R$11–R$22 ($5–$10). Although some airports accept credit cards as payment for departure taxes, it's wise to **have the appropriate amount in reais.**

FLYING TIMES

The flying time from New York is 8½ hours, from Miami, it's seven hours. Most flights from Los Angeles go through Miami and take 12 hours. From London, it's seven hours to São Paulo. Within Brazil, it's one hour from Rio to São Paulo.

RECONFIRMING

Always **reconfirm your flights,** even if you have a ticket and a reservation. This is particularly true for travel within Brazil and throughout South America, where flights tend to operate at full capacity—usually with passengers who have a great deal of baggage to process before departure.

Bus Travel to and from Rio

Regular service is available to and from Rio. Long-distance buses leave from the Rodoviária Novo Rio station, near the port. Any local bus marked RODOVIÁRIA will take you to the station. You can buy tickets at the depot or, for some destinations, from travel agents. Buses also leave from the more conveniently located Menezes Cortes Terminal, near Praça 15 de Novembro. Between Rio and São Paulo (6½–7 hours), for example, a bus departs every ½ hour and costs about R$33–R$43 ($15–$20).

When traveling by bus, **bring water, toilet paper, and an additional top layer of clothing** (the latter will come in handy if it gets cold, or it can serve as a pillow). Travel light, dress comfortably, and **keep a close watch on your belongings**—especially in bus stations.

➤ **BUS INFORMATION: Rodoviária Novo Rio station** (Av. Francisco Bicalho 1, São Cristóvão, tel. 021/2291–5151). **Menezes Cortes Terminal** (Rua São José 35, Centro, tel. 021/2533–7577).

Bus Travel Within Rio

Much has been made of the threat of being robbed on Rio's buses. However, crime has dropped significantly in the last few years; if you're discreet, you shouldn't have any problems. Just **don't wear expensive watches or jewelry, carry a camera or a map in hand, or talk boisterously in English.** It's also wise to **avoid buses during rush hour.**

CityRio, run by Riotur, takes you to 270 sightseeing points—including the beaches—in air-conditioned comfort. Tickets are R$16, R$30, or R$40 for 24-, 36-, or 48-hour passes. Buses operate from 8 to 6, at half-hour intervals. A map with the schedule and description of each route in English and three other languages is available.

Local buses are inexpensive and can take you anywhere you want to go. (Route maps aren't available, but the tourist office has lists of routes to the most popular sights.) You **enter buses at the rear,** where you pay an attendant and pass through a turnstile, then exit at the front. **Have your fare in hand when you board** to avoid flashing bills or wallets. Be aware that bus drivers speak no English, and they drive like maniacs.

The upscale, privately run, and air-conditioned frescão buses run between the beaches, downtown, and Rio's two airports. These vehicles, which look like highway buses, stop at regular bus stops but also may be flagged down wherever you see them. Also recommended are the *jardineira* buses, open-sided vehicles (they look like old-fashioned streetcars) that follow the beach drive from Copacabana to São Conrado as well as beyond to Barra da Tijuca. White posts along the street mark jardineira stops. They offer excellent views of the scenery and drive slowly along the beach avenue, a welcome relief to anyone who has ridden the regular city buses. Green minivans also run back and forth along beachfront avenues, stopping to pick up and drop off people wherever they're flagged. (Fares start at about R$5.)

➤ **BUS INFORMATION: CityRio** (tel. 0800/225–8060).

Cameras & Photography

Brazil, with its majestic landscapes and varied cityscapes, is a photographer's dream. Brazilians seem amenable to having picture-taking visitors in their midst, but you should always **ask permission before taking pictures in churches or of individuals.**

If you plan to take photos on some of the city's many beaches, **bring a skylight (81B or 81C) or polarizing filter** to minimize haze and light problems.

FILM

Bring your own film. It's expensive in Brazil and is frequently stored in hot conditions. Plan on shooting a minimum of one 36-exposure roll per week of travel.

Car Rental

Car rentals can be arranged through hotels or agencies and cost about R$80–R$226 a day for standard models. Agencies include Hertz and Unidas. Both also have desks at the international and domestic airports.

➤ **MAJOR AGENCY: Hertz** (Av. Princesa Isabel 334, Copacabana, tel. 021/2275–7440; Aeroporto Internacional Antônio Carlos Jobim, tel. 021/3398–4338; Aeroporto Santos Dumont, tel. 021/2262–0612).

➤ **LOCAL AGENCIES: Localiza Rent a Car** (Av. Princesa Isabel 214, Copacabana, tel. 021/2275–3340; Aeroporto Internacional Antônio Carlos Jobim, tel. 021/3398–5445; Aeroporto Santos Dumont, tel. 021/2533–2677). **Unidas** (Av. Princesa Isabel 350, Copacabana, tel. 021/2275–8299).

INSURANCE

When driving a rented car you are generally responsible for any damage to or loss of the vehicle as well as for any property damage or personal injury that you may cause. Before you rent, see what coverage your personal auto-insurance policy and credit cards provide.

REQUIREMENTS & RESTRICTIONS

In Brazil, the minimum driving age is 18. In theory, foreign driver's licenses are acceptable. In practice, however, police (particularly highway police) have been known to claim that driving with a foreign license is a violation in order to shake down drivers for bribes. It's best to **get an international driver's license,** which is seldom challenged. If you do plan to drive in Brazil, find out in advance from a car rental agency what type of proof of insurance you need to carry.

SURCHARGES

Before you pick up a car in one city and leave it in another, **ask about drop-off charges or one-way service fees,** which can be substantial. Note, too, that some rental agencies charge extra if you return the car before the time specified in your contract. To avoid a hefty refueling fee, **fill the tank just before you turn in the car,** but be aware that gas stations near the rental outlet may overcharge.

Car Travel

The carioca style of driving is passionate to the point of abandon: traffic jams are common, the streets aren't well marked, and red lights are often more decorative than functional. Despite new parking areas along the beachfront boulevards, finding a spot can still be a problem. If you do choose to drive, exercise extreme caution, wear seat belts at all times, and keep the doors locked.

Turismo Clássico Travel, one of the country's most reliable travel and transport agencies, can arrange for a driver, with or without an English-speaking guide (four hours with a driver only is R$200). Classico's owners, Liliana and Vera, speak English, and each has 20 years of experience in organizing transportation—often working with film crews. They also offer sightseeing tours.

➤ **CONTACTS: Turismo Clássico Travel** (Av. Nossa Senhora de Copacabana 1059, Sala 805, Copacabana, tel. 021/2523–3390).

EMERGENCY SERVICES

The Automóvel Clube do Brasil (Automobile Club of Brazil) provides emergency assistance to foreign motorists in cities and on highways, but only if they're members of an automobile club in their own nation.

➤ **CONTACT: Automóvel Clube do Brasil** (Rua do Passeio 90, Rio de Janeiro, tel. 021/2240–4060 or 021/2240–4191).

GASOLINE

Gasoline in Brazil costs around R$1.90 (88¢) a liter. Unleaded gas, called *especial*, costs about the same. Brazil also has an extensive fleet of ethanol-powered cars. Ethanol fuel is sold at all gas stations and is priced a little less than gasoline. However, such cars get lower mileage, so they offer little advantage over gas-powered cars.

There's a gas station on every main street in Rio: for example, on Avenida Atlântica in Copacabana; around the Lagoa Rodrigo de

Freitas and at Avenida Vieira Souto in Ipanema. International companies, such as Shell and Esso, are represented. The gas stations run by Brazilian oil company Petrobras are called BR. Ipiranga is another local option. Half of the gas stations are open from 6 AM until 10 PM and the other half are open 24 hours with convenience stores. As gas stations don't have emergency service, it's better to ask if car-rental insurance includes it.

➤ **GAS STATIONS: BR** (Posto de Gasolina Cardeal: Av. Atlântica s/n, Leme, tel. 021/2275–5696; Posto Santa Clara: Av. Atlântica s/n, Copacabana, tel. 021/2547–1467). **Ipiranga** (Ponei Posto de Gasolina: Av. Borges de Medeiros 3151, Lagoa, tel. 021/2539–1283).

PARKING

Finding a space is a major task. It's best to **head for a garage or a lot** and leave your car with the attendant. Should you find a space on the street, you'll probably have to pay a fee. There are no meters; instead, there's a system involving coupons that allow you to park for a certain time period (usually two hours) and that you post in your car's window. You can buy them from uniformed street-parking attendants or at newsstands.

No-parking zones are marked by a crossed-out capital letter E (which means *estacionamento*, the Portuguese word for "parking"). These zones are, more often than not, filled with cars, which are rarely bothered by the police.

RULES OF THE ROAD

Brazilians drive on the right, and in general, traffic laws are the same as those in the United States. The use of seat belts is mandatory. The national speed limit is 80 kph (48 mph) but is seldom observed. If you do get a ticket for some sort of violation—real or imagined—don't argue. And plan to spend longer than you want settling it.

Children in Brazil

Brazilians love children, and having yours along may prove to be your ticket to meeting locals. Children are welcomed in hotels and restaurants, especially on weekends, when Brazilian families go out for brunch or lunch in droves.

Large hotels often offer a range of supervised activities—picnics, movies, classes, contests—for children of all ages. Brazil is a country of a great cultural diversity, so try to **attend one of the many festivals** held all over the country throughout the year. These often feature music and dance performances that transcend language barriers and will acquaint children with Brazilian folklore. Older kids and teenagers may well be captivated by Brazil's plants and animals. **Take a guided tour of an urban park or a trek into a national preserve.** Such expeditions are a safe, easy way to experience nature.

If you are renting a car, don't forget to **arrange for a car seat** when you reserve. For general advice about traveling with children, check out *Fodor's FYI: Travel with Your Baby* (available in bookstores everywhere).

PRECAUTIONS

Any person under the age of 18 who isn't traveling with both parents or legal guardian(s) must provide a notarized letter of consent signed by the nonaccompanying parent or guardian. The notarized letter must be authenticated by the Brazilian embassy or consulate and translated into Portuguese.

Children must have all their inoculations up to date (those between the ages of three months and six years must have an international polio vaccination certificate) before leaving home.

SIGHTS & ATTRACTIONS

Places that are especially appealing to children are indicated by a rubber-duckie icon ( ) in the margin.

SUPPLIES & EQUIPMENT

You'll find international brands of baby formula (*leite nan*) and diapers (*fraldas*) in drugstores, supermarkets, and convenience shops. The average cost of a 450-gram (16-ounce) container of formula is R$9 ($4). The average price for a package of diapers is R$9 ($4).

Consulates

➤ **CONTACTS: Australia** (Av. Rio Branco 1, Room 810, Centro, tel. 021/2518–3351). **Canada** (Rua Lauro Müller 116, Room 1104, Botafogo, tel. 021/2542–7593). **United Kingdom** (Praia do Flamengo 284, 2nd floor, Flamengo, tel. 021/2553–6850). **United States** (Av. Presidente Wilson 147, Centro, tel. 021/2292–7117).

Computers on the Road

If you're traveling with a laptop, carry a spare battery, a universal adapter plug, and a converter if your computer isn't dual voltage. **Ask about electrical surges** before plugging in your computer. **Keep your disks out of the sun** and **avoid excessive heat for both your computer and disks.** In Brazil, carrying a laptop computer signals wealth and could make you a target for thieves; **conceal your laptop in a generic bag, and keep it close to you at all times.**

Internet access is surprisingly widespread. In addition to business centers in luxury hotels and full-fledged cybercafés, look for computers set up in telephone offices. Rates range from R$6.50 ($3) to R$22 ($10) an hour. Dial-up speeds are variable, though they tend toward the sluggish.

Customs & Duties

When shopping, **keep receipts** for all purchases. Upon reentering the country, **be ready to show customs officials what you've bought.** If you feel a duty is incorrect or object to the way your clearance was handled, note the inspector's badge number and ask to see a supervisor. If the problem isn't resolved, write to the appropriate authorities, beginning with the port director at your point of entry.

IN BRAZIL

Formerly strict import controls have been substantially liberalized as part of the Brazilian government's efforts to open up the nation's economy. In addition to personal items, you're now permitted to bring in, duty-free, up to R$1,085 ($500) worth of gifts purchased abroad, including up to 2 liters of liquor. If you plan to bring in plants, you may do so only with documentation authenticated by the consular service.

IN AUSTRALIA

Australian residents who are 18 or older may bring home $A400 worth of souvenirs and gifts (including jewelry), 250 cigarettes or 250 grams of tobacco, and 1,125 ml of alcohol (including wine, beer, and spirits). Residents under 18 may bring back $A200 worth of goods. Prohibited items include meat products. Seeds, plants, and fruits need to be declared upon arrival.

➤ **INFORMATION: Australian Customs Service** (Regional Director, Box 8, Sydney, NSW 2001, Australia, tel. 02/9213–2000, fax 02/9213–4000, www.customs.gov.au).

IN CANADA

Canadian residents who have been out of Canada for at least seven days may bring home C$500 worth of goods duty-free. If you've been away fewer than seven days but more than 48 hours, the duty-free allowance drops to C$200; if your trip lasts 24–48 hours, the allowance is C$50. You may not pool allowances with family members. Goods claimed under the C$500 exemption may follow you by mail; those claimed under the lesser exemptions must accompany you. Alcohol and tobacco products may be included in the seven-day and 48-hour exemptions but not in the 24-hour exemption. If you meet the age requirements of the province or territory through which you reenter Canada, you may bring in, duty-free, 1.14 liters (40 imperial ounces) of wine or liquor *or* 24 12-ounce cans or bottles of beer or ale. If you are 16 or older you may bring in, duty-free, 200 cigarettes and 50 cigars. Check ahead of time with Revenue Canada or the Department of Agriculture for policies regarding meat products, seeds, plants, and fruits.

You may send an unlimited number of gifts worth up to C$60 each duty-free to Canada. Label the package UNSOLICITED GIFT—VALUE UNDER $60. Alcohol and tobacco are excluded.

➤ **INFORMATION: Revenue Canada** (2265 St. Laurent Blvd. S, Ottawa, Ontario K1G 4K3, Canada, tel. 613/993–0534; 800/461–9999 in Canada, fax 613/991–4126, www.ccra-adrc.gc.ca).

IN NEW ZEALAND

Homeward-bound residents 17 or older may bring back NZ$700 worth of souvenirs and gifts. Your duty-free allowance also includes 4.5 liters of wine or beer; one 1,125-ml bottle of spirits; and either 200 cigarettes, 250 grams of tobacco, 50 cigars, or a combination of the three up to 250 grams. Prohibited items include meat products, seeds, plants, and fruits.

➤ **INFORMATION: New Zealand Customs** (Custom House, 50 Anzac Ave., Box 29, Auckland, New Zealand, tel. 09/300–5399, fax 09/359–6730, www.customs.govt.nz).

IN THE U.K.

From countries outside the EU, including Brazil, you may bring home, duty-free, 200 cigarettes or 50 cigars; 1 liter of spirits or 2 liters of fortified or sparkling wine or liqueurs; 2 liters of still table wine; 60 ml of perfume; 250 ml of toilet water; plus £136 worth of other goods, including gifts and souvenirs. If returning from outside the EU, prohibited items include meat products, seeds, plants, and fruits.

➤ **INFORMATION: HM Customs and Excise** (St. Christopher House, Southwark, London, SE1 OTE, U.K., tel. 020/7928–3344, tel. 020/7202–4227, www.hmce.gov.uk).

IN THE U.S.

U.S. residents who have been out of the country for at least 48 hours (and who have not used the US$400 allowance or any part of it in the past 30 days) may bring home US$400 worth of foreign goods duty-free.

U.S. residents 21 and older may bring back 1 liter of alcohol duty-free. In addition, regardless of your age, you are allowed 200 cigarettes and 100 non-Cuban cigars. Antiques, which the U.S. Customs Service defines as objects more than 100 years old, enter duty-free, as do original works of art done entirely by hand, including paintings, drawings, and sculptures.

You may also mail or ship packages home duty-free: up to US$200 worth of goods for personal use, with a limit of one parcel per addressee per day (except alcohol or tobacco products or perfume worth more than US$5); label the package PERSONAL USE and attach a list of its contents and their retail value. Do not label the package UNSOLICITED GIFT or your duty-free exemption will drop to US$100. Mailed items do not affect your duty-free allowance on your return.

Dining

Eating is a national passion, and portions are huge. In many restaurants, plates are prepared for two people; when you order, ask if one plate will suffice. In addition, some restaurants automatically bring a *couberto* (an appetizer course of such items as bread, cheese or pâté, olives, quail eggs, and the like). You'll be charged extra for this, and you're perfectly within your rights to send it back if you don't want it.

The restaurants (all of which are indicated by a ✕) that we list are the cream of the crop in each price category. Properties indicated by a are lodging establishments whose restaurant warrants a special trip.

MEALTIMES

You'll be hard-pressed to find breakfast outside a hotel restaurant. At lunch and dinner, portions are large. In Rio, lunch and dinner are served later than in the United States. In restaurants, lunch usually starts around 1 and can last until 3. Dinner is always eaten after 8 and, in many cases, not until 10.

RESERVATIONS & DRESS

Reservations are always a good idea: we mention them only when they're essential or not accepted. Book as far ahead as you can, and reconfirm as soon as you arrive. We mention dress only when men are required to wear a jacket or a jacket and tie.

Disabilities & Accessibility

Although international chain hotels in large cities have some suitable rooms and facilities and it's easy to hire private cars and drivers for excursions, Brazil isn't very well equipped to handle travelers with disabilities. There are few ramps and curb cuts, and it takes effort and planning to negotiate.

Some areas on the south side of Rio *do* have ramps and wide sidewalks with even surfaces. Legislation concerning people with disabilities has been approved but has yet to be enforced. There's no central clearinghouse for information on this topic, so the best local resource is the staff at your hotel.

Electricity

The current in Rio is 110 or 120 volts, 60 cycles alternating current (the same as in the United States and Canada). **Bring a converter.**

Wall outlets take Continental-type plugs, with two round prongs. **Consider buying a universal adapter;** the Swiss Army knife of adapters, a universal has several types of plugs in one handy unit. If your appliances are dual-voltage (as many laptops are), you'll need only an adapter. Don't use 110-volt outlets, marked FOR SHAVERS ONLY, for high-wattage appliances such as blow-dryers.

Emergencies

➤ **EMERGENCY SERVICES: Ambulance and Fire** (tel. 193). **Police** (tel. 190). **Tourism Police** (Av. Afrânio de Melo Franco, Leblon, tel. 021/3399–7170).

➤ **PRIVATE MEDICAL CLINICS: Cardio Plus** (Rua Visconde de Pirajá 330, Ipanema, tel. 021/2521–4899). **Galdino Campos Cardio Copa Medical Clinic** (Av. Nossa Senhora de Copacabana 492, Copacabana, tel. 021/2548–9966). **Medtur** (Av. Nossa Senhora de Copacabana 647, Copacabana, tel. 021/2235–3339). **Policlínica Barata Ribeiro** (Rua Barata Ribeiro 51, Copacabana, tel. 021/2275–4697).

➤ **24-HOUR PHARMACIES: Drogaria Pacheco** (Av. Nossa Senhora de Copacabana 534, Copacabana, tel. 021/2548–1525). **Farmácia do Leme** (Av. Prado Junior 237, Leme, tel. 021/2275–3847).

English-Language Media

Outside the programs on cable TV in large chain hotels, you'll be hard-pressed to find anything in English. In movie theaters, some British and American films are shown in English with Portuguese subtitles. In major cities, large newsstands and bookstores sell most American and a few British publications—albeit at prices much higher than you would pay at home. Bookstores that carry some English-language publications include Letras & Expressões, Livraria Argumento, Livraria Kosmos, and Sodiler.

➤ **BOOKSTORES: Letras & Expressões** (Rua Visconde de Pirajá 276, Ipanema, tel. 021/2521–6110). **Livraria Argumento** (Rua Dias Ferreira 417, Leblon, tel. 021/2239–5294). **Livraria Kosmos**

(Rua do Rosário 155, Centro, tel. 021/2224–8616). **Sodiler** (Aeroporto Internacional Antônio Carlos Jobim, tel. 021/3393–9511; Aeroporto Santos Dumont, tel. 021/3393–4377).

➤ **NEWSSTANDS: Banca General Osório** (corner of Praça General Osório and Rua Jangadeiros, Ipanema, tel. 021/2287–9248). **Banca Nossa Senhora da Paz** (Rua Visconde de Pirajá 365, Ipanema, tel. 021/2522–0880).

Etiquette & Behavior

Although Brazil is a predominately Catholic country—people dress nicely to enter churches, and hats are frowned upon during mass—in many places, especially Rio, there's an anything-goes outlook.

Whether they tend toward the conservative or the risqué, Brazilians are a very friendly lot. Don't be afraid to smile in the streets, ask for directions, or strike up a conversation with a local (be aware, however, that a Brazilian may give you false directions before admitting that he or she doesn't know where to point you). The slower pace of life in much of the country reflects an unwavering appreciation of family and friendship (as well as a respect for the heat); knowing this will help you understand why things may take a little longer to get done.

Throughout the country, **use the thumbs-up gesture to indicate that something is OK.** The gesture created by making a circle with your thumb and index finger and holding your other fingers up in the air has a very rude meaning.

Gay & Lesbian Travel

Brazil is South America's most popular destination for gay and lesbian travelers, and Rio has numerous gay bars, organizations, and publications. Realize, however, that the acceptance of same-sex couples in the major cities may be limited to more touristy areas. Outside these destinations use discretion about public displays of affection.

The great Carnaval celebrations include many gay parades. At the end of the year, Mix Brasil International Festival of Sexual Diversity takes place in São Paulo, Rio de Janeiro and Porto Alegre.

Style Travel, an offshoot of the established Brasil Plus travel agency, is a great source of information on gay and lesbian lodging, tour, and nightlife options in the area. They can also supply knowledgeable, English-speaking gay and lesbian guides and arrange trips to outlying areas. Style Travel is a member of the International Gay and Lesbian Travel Association (IGLTA).

G Magazine is Rio's gay and lesbian glossy magazine. It's available at most newsstands and lists local arts, music, and style events—in Portuguese. Visit Rio's on-line "Gay Guide" at www.ipanema.com/rio/gay. The site is a wealth of information—from the practical to the downright sexy. Rio's gay beach scene is at Bolsa, on Copacabana Beach in front of the Copacabana Palace, and at Ipanema by Posts 8 and 9, east of Rua Farme de Amoedo, a.k.a. Farme Gay. Locals on these sandy stretches are usually open to questions about what's happening in the gay and lesbian community.

➤ **CONTACTS: Grupo Arco-Íris de Conscientização Homossexual** (tel. 021/2552–5995, 021/9295–7229). **Style Travel** (Rua Visconde de Pirajá 433, 6th floor, Ipanema, tel. 021/2247–8915 or 021/2522–0709).

Health

FOOD & DRINK

You should avoid tap water (note that ice in restaurants and bars is safe as it's usually made from bottled water).

MEDICAL PLANS

No one plans to get sick while traveling, but it happens, so **consider signing up with a medical-assistance company.** Members get doctor referrals, emergency evacuation or repatriation, hot lines for medical consultation, cash for emergencies, and other assistance.

➤ **MEDICAL-ASSISTANCE COMPANIES: International SOS Assistance** (www.internationalsos.com; 8 Neshaminy Interplex, Suite 207, Trevose, PA 19053, tel. 215/245–4707 or 800/523–6586, fax 215/244–9617; 12 Chemin Riantbosson, 1217 Meyrin 1, Geneva, Switzerland, tel. 4122/785–6464, fax 4122/785–6424; 331 N. Bridge Rd., 17-00, Odeon Towers, Singapore 188720, tel. 65/338–7800, fax 65/338–7611).

OVER-THE-COUNTER REMEDIES

Mild cases of diarrhea may respond to Imodium (known generically as loperamide) or Pepto-Bismol (not as strong), both of which can be purchased over the counter. Drink plenty of purified water or *chá* (tea)—*camomila* (chamomile) is a good folk remedy. In severe cases, rehydrate yourself with a salt–sugar solution: ½ teaspoon *sal* (salt) and 4 tablespoons *açúcar* (sugar) per quart of *agua* (water). The word for aspirin is *aspirinha*; Tylenol is pronounced *tee*-luh-nawl.

PESTS & OTHER HAZARDS

Sunshine, limes, and skin don't mix well. The oil in lime-skin juice, if left on human skin and exposed to the sun, will burn and scar. If you're using lime and will be exposed to a lot of sun, be sure to wash well with soap and water. Should spots appear on skin areas that have been exposed, pharmacies will know which creams work best to heal the burns. (Note that affected areas shouldn't be exposed to the sun for three months following the burn.)

Heatstroke and heat prostration are common though easily preventable maladies. The symptoms for either can vary but always start with headaches, nausea, and dizziness. If ignored, these symptoms can worsen until you require medical attention. In hot weather be sure to **rehydrate regularly, wear loose, lightweight clothing, and avoid overexerting yourself.**

Aside from the obvious safe-sex precautions, keep in mind that Brazil's blood supply isn't subject to the same intense screening as it is in North America, western Europe, Australia, or New Zealand. If you need a transfusion and circumstances permit it, ask that the blood be screened. Insulin-dependent diabetics or those who require injections should pack enough of the appropriate supplies—syringes, needles, disinfectants—to last the trip. In addition, you might want to resist the temptation to get a new tattoo or body piercing while you're in Brazil.

SHOTS & MEDICATIONS

All travelers should have up-to-date tetanus boosters, and a hepatitis A inoculation can prevent one of the most common intestinal infections. If you're heading to tropical regions, you should get yellow fever shots, particularly if you're traveling overland from a country where yellow fever has been prevalent, such as Peru or Bolivia. Children must have current inoculations against measles, mumps, rubella, and polio.

According to the Centers for Disease Control (CDC) there's a limited risk of contracting cholera, typhoid, malaria, hepatitis B, dengue, and chagas.

In areas with malaria and dengue, which are both carried by mosquitoes, take mosquito nets, wear clothing that covers the body, apply repellent containing DEET, and use a spray against flying insects in living and sleeping areas.

Dengue has become an increasing problem in the Amazon and Pantanal regions. Unlike malaria, it's primarily a concern in urban areas and is spread by mosquitoes that are more active during the day than at night. No vaccine exists against dengue.

➤ **HEALTH WARNINGS: National Centers for Disease Control and Prevention** (CDC; National Center for Infectious Diseases, Division of Quarantine, Traveler's Health Section, 1600 Clifton Rd. NE, M/S E-03, Atlanta, GA 30333, tel. 888/232–3228 or 800/311–3435, fax 888/232–3299, www.cdc.gov).

Holidays

Major national holidays include: New Year's Day (Jan. 1); Epiphany (Jan. 6); Carnaval, the week preceding Ash Wednesday (which falls on Feb. 13 in 2002 and Mar. 5 in 2003); Good Friday (Mar. 29, 2002; Apr. 18, 2003); Easter (Mar. 31, 2002; Apr. 20, 2003); Tiradentes Day (Apr. 21); Labor Day (May 1); Corpus Christi (May 30, 2002; June 9, 2003); Independence Day (Sept. 7); Our Lady of Aparecida Day (Oct. 12); All Souls' Day (Nov. 1); Declaration of the Republic Day (Nov. 15); Christmas (Dec. 25).

Language

The language in Brazil is Portuguese, not Spanish, and Brazilians will appreciate it if you know the difference. The two languages are distinct, but common origins mean that many words are similar, and fluent speakers of Spanish will be able to make themselves understood. English is spoken among educated Brazilians and, in general, by at least some of the staff at hotels, tour operators, and travel agencies. Store clerks and waiters may have a smattering of English; taxi and bus drivers won't. As in many places throughout the world, you're more likely to find English-speaking locals in major cities than in small towns or the countryside.

Lodging

When you consider your lodgings in Brazil, add these three terms to your vocabulary: *pousada* (inn), *fazenda* (farm), and "flat" or "block" hotel (apartment-hotel). Flat hotels are popular with Brazilians, particularly in cities and with families and groups. Some have amenities such as pools, but for most folks, the biggest draw is affordability: with kitchen facilities and room for a group, flat hotels offer more for the money.

If you ask for a double room, you'll get a room for two people, but you're not guaranteed a double mattress. If you'd like to avoid twin beds, **ask for a *cama de casal*** ("couple's bed"; no wedding ring seems to be required).

The lodgings (all indicated with a) that we list are the cream of the crop in each price category. We always list the facilities that are available—but we don't specify whether they cost extra: when pricing accommodations, always ask what's included. All hotels listed have private bath unless otherwise noted. Properties indicated by a are lodging establishments whose restaurant warrants a special trip.

Assume that hotels operate on the European Plan (**EP,** with no meals) unless we specify that they're all-inclusive (including all meals and most activities) or use the Breakfast Plan (**BP,** with a full breakfast daily), Continental Plan (**CP,** with a Continental breakfast daily), Full American Plan (**FAP,** with all meals), or Modified American Plan (**MAP,** with breakfast and dinner daily).

HOSTELS

No matter what your age, you can **save on lodging costs by staying at hostels.** There are about 100 hostels scattered across Brazil, all of them affiliated with Hostelling International (HI). Many Brazilian hostels' names are preceded by the letters AJ (Albergues de Juventude). The Federação Brasileira dos Albergues de Juventude (FBJA; Brazilian Federation of Youth Hostels) is based in Rio.

➤ **ORGANIZATIONS: Federação Brasileira dos Albergues de Juventude** (Rua da Assembleia 10, Sala 1211, Centro, Rio De Janeiro, RJ 20011, tel. 021/2531–2234 or 021/2531–1302).

HOTELS

Hotels listed with EMBRATUR, Brazil's national tourist board, are rated using stars. Note, however, that the number of stars awarded appears to be based strictly on the number of amenities, without taking into account intangibles such as service and atmosphere.

Carnaval (Carnival), the year's principal festival, occurs during the four days preceding Ash Wednesday. For top hotels in Rio, you must **make reservations a year in advance.** Hotel rates rise 20% on average for Carnaval. Not as well known outside Brazil but equally impressive is Rio's New Year's Eve celebration. More than a million people gather along Copacabana Beach for a massive fireworks display and to honor the sea goddess Iemanjá. To ensure a room, **book at least six months in advance.**

Hotels accept credit cards for payment, but first ask if there's a discount for cash. Try to bargain hard for a cash-on-the barrel discount, then pay in local currency.

Mail & Shipping

The main post office is in Centro, but there are branches all over the city, including one at Galeão, several on Avenida Nossa Senhora de Copacabana in Copacabana, and one on Rua Visconde de Pirajá in Ipanema. Most are open weekdays 8–5 and Saturday 8–noon.

Federal Express and DHL have offices here that are open weekdays, but shipping usually takes longer than just overnight. You can call a day ahead to schedule pick-up.

➤ **COURIER SERVICES: DHL** (Rua Teófilo Otoni 15 A, Centro, tel. 021/2263–5454). **Federal Express** (Av. Calógeras 23, Centro, tel. 021/2262–8565).

➤ **POST OFFICE: Main Branch** (Av. Presidente Vargas 3077, tel. 021/2503–8222).

RECEIVING MAIL

Mail can be addressed to "poste restante" and sent to any major post office. The address must include the code for that particular branch. American Express will hold mail for its cardholders.

Metrô Travel

Rio's subway system, the metrô, is clean, relatively safe, and efficient—a delight to use—but it's not comprehensive. Reaching sights distant from metrô stations can be a challenge, especially in summer when the infamous carioca traffic fans what is already 90-degree exasperation. Plan your tours accordingly; tourism offices and some metrô stations have maps.

Trains run daily from 6 AM to 11 PM along two lines: Linha 1 runs north from the Cardeal Arcoverde stop in Copacabana, parallel to the coast and into downtown, then west to its terminus at Saens Pena station; Linha 2 starts four stops before Saens Pena at Estácio and heads northwest to Rio's edge at the Pavuna station. A single metrô ticket costs R$1, a 10-pack is R$10 (but there are discounts for riding the subway during the nonrush hours, between noon and 4). Combination metrô-bus tickets allow you to take special buses to and from the Botafogo station: the M-21 runs to Leblon via Jardim Botânico and Jóquei; the M-22 goes to Leblon by way of Túnel Velho, Copacabana, and Ipanema.

➤ **METRÔ INFORMATION: Information Line** (tel. 021/2292–6116 or 021/2255–5552).

Money Matters

Prices throughout this guide are given for adults. Substantially reduced fees are almost always available for children, students, and senior citizens.

Top hotels in Rio go for more than R$430 ($200) a night, and meals can—but do not have to—cost as much. Self-service salad bars where you pay by weight (per kilo, about 2.2 pounds) are inexpensive alternatives everywhere, though be sure to choose carefully among them. Taxis can be pricey. City buses, subways, and long-distance buses are all inexpensive; plane fares aren't.

ATMS

Nearly all the nation's major banks have automated teller machines. MasterCard and Cirrus are rarely accepted (some airport Banco Itau ATMs are linked to Cirrus); Visa and Plus cards are. American Express card holders can make withdrawals at most Bradesco ATMs marked 24 HORAS. To be on the safe side, carry a variety of cards. Note also that if your PIN is more than four digits long and/or uses letters instead of numbers, it might not work; talk to your bank. Finally, for your card to function on some ATMs, you may need to hit a screen command (perhaps, *estrangeiro*) if you are a foreign client.

CURRENCY

Brazil's unit of currency is the real (R$; plural: *reais*, though it's sometimes seen as *reals*). One real has 100 centavos (cents). There are notes worth 1, 5, 10, 50, and 100 reais, together with coins worth 1, 5, 10, 25, and 50 centavos, and 1 real, all of which feel and look similar.

CURRENCY EXCHANGE

At press time, the real was at 3.08 to the pound sterling, 2.15 to the U.S. dollar, 1.37 to the Canadian dollar, 1.07 to the Australia dollar, and 0.89 to the New Zealand dollar.

Generally, exchange rates are better in the city than at the airport and cash gets better rates than traveler's checks. Most Brazilian banks don't exchange money. One that does is Banco do Brasil. The branch at Galeão offers good exchange rates, but it won't provide credit-card advances.

Casas do câmbio (exchange houses) are found all over the city, especially along the beaches and on Avenida Nossa Senhora de Copacabana and Rua Visconde de Pirajá in Ipanema. Many change money without charging a service fee. Sometimes, depending on the amount of money you wish to exchange, exchange houses have a better rate than the banks. American Express is another option.

Some hotels, such as the Caesar Park and the Copacabana Palace, offer competitive rates but will charge a commission if you're not a guest there. On weekends, hotels may be your best bet because few other places are open. Or try the automatic-teller machines (ATMs) throughout town that dispense reais.

➤ **BANKS: Banco do Brasil** (Rua Bartolomeu Mitre 438 A, Leblon, tel. 021/2512–2999; Av. Nossa Senhora de Copacabana 594, tel. 021/2548–8992; Aeroporto Internacional Antônio Carlos Jobim, third floor, tel. 021/3398–3652). **Banco 24 Horas ATM** (Av. Nossa Senhora de Copacabana 202; Av. Nossa Senhora de Copacabana 599; Av. Nossa Senhora de Copacabana 1366; Visconde de Pirajá 174, Ipanema).

➤ **EXCHANGE SERVICES: American Express** (Av. Atlântica 1702 B, Copacabana, tel. 021/2548–2148 or 0800/778–5050.) **Casa Universal** (Av. Nossa Senhora de Copacabana 371 E, Copacabana, tel. 021/2548–6696).

Packing

If you're doing business in Brazil, you'll need the same attire you would wear in U.S. and European cities: for men, suits and ties; for women, suits for day wear and cocktail dresses or the like for an evening out. For sightseeing, casual clothing and good walking shoes are appropriate; most restaurants don't require very formal attire. For beach vacations, you'll need lightweight sportswear, a bathing suit, a beach cover-up, a sun hat, and really good sunscreen.

Passports & Visas

When traveling internationally, **carry your passport** even if you don't need one (it's always the best form of I.D.) and **make two photocopies of the data page** (one for someone at home and another for you, carried separately from your passport). If you lose your passport, promptly call the nearest embassy or consulate and the local police.

ENTERING BRAZIL

To enter Brazil, all U.S. citizens, even infants, must have both a passport and a tourist visa (valid for five years). To obtain one, you must submit the following to the Brazilian embassy or to the nearest consulate: a passport that will be valid for six months past the date of first entry to Brazil; a passport-type photo; a photocopy of your round-trip ticket or a signed letter from a travel agency with confirmed round-trip bookings or proof of your ability to pay for your stay in Brazil; and cash, a money order, or a certified check for US$45 (there's also a US$10 handling fee if anyone other than the applicant submits the visa).

If you're a business traveler, you may need a business visa (valid for 90 days). It has all the same requirements as a tourist visa, but you'll also need a letter on company letterhead—addressed to the embassy or consulate and signed by an authorized representative (other than you)—stating the nature of your business in Brazil, itinerary, business contacts, dates of arrival and departure, and that the company assumes all financial and moral responsibility while you're in Brazil. The fee is US$105 (plus the US$10 fee if someone other than you submits the visa). In addition to the forms of payment detailed above, a company check is also acceptable.

Canadian nationals, Australians, and New Zealanders also need visas to enter the country. For Canadians, the fee is C$40; for New Zealanders, NZ$20; and for Australians, there's no charge. Citizens of the United Kingdom don't need a visa.

In the United States there are consulates in Atlanta, Boston, Chicago, Houston, Los Angeles, Miami, New York, San Francisco, and San Juan. To get the location of the Brazilian consulate to which you must apply, contact the Brazilian embassy. Note that some consulates don't allow you to apply for a visa by mail. If you don't live near a city with a consulate, consider hiring a concierge-type service to do your legwork. Many cities have these companies, which not only help with the paperwork for such things as visas and passports but also send someone to wait in line for you.

Rest Rooms

The word for "bathroom" is *banheiro,* though the term *sanitários* (toilets) is also used. *Homens* means "men" and *mulheres* means "women." Around major tourist attractions and along the main beaches in big cities, you'll find public rest rooms. In other areas you may have to rely on the kindness of local restaurant and shop owners. If a smile and polite request ("*Por favor, posso usar o banheiro?*") don't work, become a customer—the purchase of a drink or a knickknack might just buy you a trip to the bathroom. Rest areas with relatively clean, well-equipped bathrooms are plentiful along major highways. Still, carry a pocket-size package of tissues in case there's no toilet paper. Bathroom attendants will *truly* appreciate a tip of a few spare centavos.

Safety

Despite Rio's reputation, crime is no more likely than in any large city. Most crimes involving visitors occur in crowded public areas: beaches, busy sidewalks, intersections, and city buses. Pickpockets, usually children, work in groups. One will distract you while another grabs a wallet, bag, or camera. **Be particularly wary of children who thrust themselves in front of you and ask for money** or offer to shine your shoes. Another member of the gang may strike from behind, grabbing your valuables and disappearing into the crowd.

Another tactic is for criminals to approach your car at intersections. Always **keep doors locked and windows partially closed.** Leave valuables in your hotel safe, don't wear expensive jewelry or watches, and keep cameras out of sight. Walking alone at night on the beach isn't a good idea; neither is getting involved with drugs—penalties for possession are severe, and dealers are the worst of the worst.

Note that Brazilian law requires everyone to have official identification with them at all times. **Carry a copy of your passport's data page and of the Brazilian visa stamp** (leave the actual passport in the hotel safe).

WOMEN IN BRAZIL

Although women are gradually assuming a more important role in the nation's job force, machismo is still a strong part of Brazilian culture. Stares and catcalls aren't uncommon. Although you should have no fear of traveling unaccompanied, you should still take a few precautions.

Ask your hotel staff to recommend a reliable cab company, and **call for a taxi instead of hailing one on the street,** especially at night. **Dress to avoid unwanted attention.** For example, always wear a cover-up when heading to or from the beach. **Avoid eye contact** with unsavory individuals. If such a person approaches you, discourage him by politely but firmly by saying, "*Por favor, me dê licença*" ("Excuse me, please") and then walk away with resolve.

Senior-Citizen Travel

There's no reason why active, well-traveled senior citizens shouldn't visit Brazil, whether on an independent (but prebooked) vacation, an escorted tour, or an adventure vacation. The country is full of good hotels and competent ground operators who will meet your flights and organize your sightseeing. Before you leave home, however, determine what medical services your health insurance will cover outside the United States; note that Medicare doesn't provide for payment of hospital and medical services outside the United States. If you need additional travel insurance, buy it.

To qualify for age-related discounts, **mention your senior-citizen status up front** when booking hotel reservations (not when checking out) and before you're seated in restaurants (not when paying the bill). When renting a car, ask about promotional car-rental discounts, which can be cheaper than senior-citizen rates.

Sightseeing Tours

You can ride around the Floresta da Tijuca and Corcovado, Angra dos Reis, or Teresópolis in renovated World War II Jeeps (1942 Dodge Commanders, Willys F-75s, and others) with the well-organized Atlantic Forest Jeep Tours. Guides speak English, French, German, and Spanish. The company also offers a range of ecological tours, including some on horseback. The superb guides at Gray Line speak your language. In addition to a variety of city tours, the company also offers trips outside town, whether you'd like to go white-water rafting on the Rio Paraíbuna, tour a coffee plantation, or spend time in Petrópolis. Helicopter tours are also an option.

Carlos Roquette is a history teacher who runs Cultural Rio, an agency that hosts trips to 8,000 destinations. Most are historic sites. A guided visit costs around R$100 per hour, depending on the size of the group. Ecology and Culture Tours offers hiking and jeep tours of Tijuca, Sugar Loaf, Santa Teresa, and various beaches. Guides speak English: morning and afternoon excursions are available. Favela Tour offers a fascinating half-day tour of two favelas. For anyone with an interest in Brazil beyond the beaches, such tours are highly recommended. The company's English-speaking guides can also be contracted for other outings.

Qualitours will take you and yours in a jeep around old Rio, the favelas, Corcovado, Floresta da Tijuca, Prainha, and Grumari. They can explain everything in English, Hungarian, French, or German. Hang glide or paraglide over Pedra da Gávea and Pedra Bonita under the supervision of São Conrado Eco-Aventura.

➤ **CONTACTS: Atlantic Forest Jeep Tours** (tel./fax 021/4495–9827, tel. 021/2495–9827). **Cultural Rio** (tel. 021/9911–3829 or 021/3322–4872, www.culturalrio.com). **Ecology and Culture Tours** (tel. 021/2522–1620). **Favela Tour** (tel. 021/3322–2727). **Gray Line** (tel. 021/2512–9919). **Qualitours** (tel. 021/2232–9710). **São Conrado Eco-Aventura** (tel. 021/2522–5586).

GUIDES

Don't hire sightseeing guides who approach you on the street. Hire one through the museum or sight you're visiting (once you get inside), a tour operator, the tourist board, your hotel, or a reputable travel agency—and no one else.

Taxes

Sales tax is included in the prices shown on goods in stores. Hotel, meal, and car rental taxes are usually tacked on in addition to the costs shown on menus and brochures. At press time, hotel taxes were roughly 5%; meal taxes, 10%; car rental taxes, 12%.

Departure taxes on international flights from Brazil aren't always included in your ticket and can run as high as R$86 ($40); domestic flights may incur a R$22 ($10) tax. Although U.S. dollars are accepted in some airports, be prepared to **pay departure taxes in reais.**

Taxis

Yellow taxis are just like those in New York, except that even fewer drivers speak English. They have meters that start at a set price and have two rates: "1" for before and "2" for after 8 PM. The "2" rate also applies to Sunday, holidays, the month of December, the neighborhoods of São Conrado and Barra da Tijuca, and when climbing steep hills. Drivers are required to post a chart noting the current fares on the inside of the left rear window. Carioca cabbies are wonderful people by and large, but there are exceptions. Remain alert and trust your instincts; a few drivers have taken nonnatives for a ride.

Radio taxis and several companies that routinely serve hotels (and whose drivers often speak English) are also options. They charge 30% more than other taxis but are reliable and, usually, air-conditioned. Other cabs working with the hotels will also charge more, normally a fixed fee that you should agree on before you leave. Reliable radio cab companies include Centro de Taxis, Coopacarioca, and Coopatur.

➤ **TAXI COMPANIES: Centro de Taxis** (tel. 021/2593–2598). **Coopacarioca** (tel. 021/2253–3847). **Coopatur** (tel. 021/2290–1009).

Telephones

Rio's area code is 021. There are public phones on corners throughout the city. They work with cards that you can buy in a variety of denominations at newsstands, banks, and some shops (some phones also work with credit cards). For long-distance calls, there are phone offices at the main bus terminal, Galeão, downtown at Praça Tiradentes 41, and in Copacabana at Avenida Nossa Senhora de Copacabana 540. To make international calls through the operator, dial 000111. For operator-assisted long-distance within Brazil, dial 101; information is 102.

LONG-DISTANCE SERVICES

AT&T, MCI, and Sprint access codes make calling long distance relatively convenient, but you may find the local access number blocked in many hotel rooms. First ask the hotel operator to connect you. If the hotel operator balks, ask for an international operator, or dial the international operator yourself. One way to improve your odds of getting connected to your long-distance carrier is to travel with more than one company's calling card (a hotel may block Sprint, for example, but not MCI). If all else fails, call from a pay phone.

Time

Rio is three hours behind GMT (Greenwich mean time), which means that if it's 5 PM in London, it's 2 PM in Rio and noon in New York.

Tipping

Note that wages can be paltry, so a little generosity can go a long way. At hotels, it can go even farther if you tip in U.S. dollars or pounds sterling (bills, not coins). At restaurants that add a 10% service charge onto the check, it's customary to give the waiter an additional 5% tip. If there's no service charge, leave 15%. In deluxe hotels, tip porters R$2 ($1) per bag, chambermaids R$2 ($1) per day, bellhops R$4–R$6 ($2–$3) for room and valet service. Tips for doormen and concierges vary, depending on the services provided. A good tip would be R$22 ($10) or higher, average R$11 ($5). For moderate and inexpensive hotels, tips tend to be minimal (salaries are so low that virtually anything is well received). If a taxi driver helps you with your luggage, a per-bag charge of about 75 centavos (35¢) is levied in addition to the fare. In general, tip taxi drivers 10% of the fare.

At the barber shop or beauty salon, a 10%–20% tip is expected. If a service station attendant does anything beyond filling up the gas tank, leave him a small tip of some spare change. Tipping in bars and cafés follows the rules of restaurants, although at outdoor bars Brazilians rarely leave a gratuity if they had only a soft drink or a beer. At airports and at train and bus stations, tip the last porter who puts your bags into the cab (R$1/50¢ a bag at airports, 50 centavos/25¢ a bag at bus and train stations). In large cities, you'll often be accosted on the street by children looking for handouts; 50 centavos (25¢) is an average "tip."

Tours & Packages

Because everything is prearranged on a prepackaged tour or independent vacation, you spend less time planning—and often get it all at a good price.

BOOKING WITH AN AGENT

Travel agents are excellent resources. But it's a good idea to collect brochures from several agencies as some agents' suggestions may be influenced by relationships with tour and package firms that reward them for volume sales. If you have a special interest, **find an agent with expertise in that area**: the American Society of Travel Agents (ASTA; ☞ Travel Agencies) has a database of specialists worldwide.

Make sure your travel agent knows the accommodations and other services of the place they're recommending. Ask about the hotel's location, room size, beds, and whether it has a pool, room service, or programs for children, if you care about these. Has your agent been there in person or sent others whom you can contact?

Do some homework on your own, too: local tourism boards can provide information about lesser-known and small-niche operators, some of which may sell only direct.

➤ **TOUR-OPERATOR RECOMMENDATIONS: American Society of Travel Agents** (☞ Travel Agencies). **National Tour Association** (NTA; 546 E. Main St., Lexington, KY 40508, tel. 859/226–4444 or 800/682–8886, www.ntaonline.com). **United States Tour Operators Association** (USTOA; 342 Madison Ave., Suite 1522, New York, NY 10173, tel. 212/599–6599 or 800/468–7862, fax 212/599–6744, www.ustoa.com).

Train Travel

Intercity trains leave from *the* central station that starred in the Oscar-nominated movie by the same name, Estação Dom Pedro II Central do Brasil. Trains, including a daily overnight train to São Paulo, also leave from the Estação Leopoldina Barao de Maria, near Praça 15 de Novembro.

➤ **TRAIN INFORMATION: Estação Dom Pedro II Central do Brasil** (Praça Cristiano Otoni on Av. President Vargas, Centro, tel. 021/2233–8818). **Estação Leopoldina Barao de Maria** (Av. Francisco Bicalho, São Cristóvão, tel. 021/2273–1122 or 021/2575–3399).

Travel Agencies

A good travel agent puts your needs first. Look for an agency that has been in business at least five years, emphasizes customer service, and has someone on staff who specializes in your destination. In addition, **make sure the agency belongs to a professional trade organization.** The American Society of Travel Agents (ASTA)—the largest and most influential in the field with more than 26,000 members in some 170 countries—maintains and enforces a strict code of ethics and will step in to help mediate any agent-client disputes if necessary. ASTA (whose motto is "Without a travel agent, you're on your own") also maintains a Web site that includes a directory of agents. (If a travel agency is also acting as your tour operator, *see* Buyer Beware in Tours & Packages.)

➤ **LOCAL AGENT REFERRALS: American Society of Travel Agents** (ASTA; tel. 800/965–2782 24-hr hot line, fax 703/739–7642, www.astanet.com). **Association of British Travel Agents** (68–71 Newman St., London W1T 3AH, U.K., tel. 020/7637–2444, fax 020/7637–0713, www.abtanet.com). **Association of Canadian Travel Agents** (130 Albert St., Ste. 1705, Ottawa, Ontario K1P 5G4, Canada, tel. 613/237–3657, fax 613/237–7502, www.acta.net). **Australian Federation of Travel Agents** (Level 3, 309 Pitt St., Sydney NSW 2000, Australia, tel. 02/9264–3299, fax 02/9264–1085, www.afta.com.au). **Travel Agents' Association of New Zealand** (Box 1888, Wellington 10033, New Zealand, tel. 04/499–0104, fax 04/499–0827, www.taanz.org.nz).

Visitor Information

The Rio de Janeiro city tourism department, Riotur, has an information booth, which is open 8–5 daily. There are also city tourism desks at the airports and the Novo Rio bus terminal. The Rio de Janeiro state tourism board, Turisrio, is open weekdays 9–6. You can also try contacting Brazil's national tourism board, Embratur.

➤ **TOURIST INFORMATION: Embratur** (Rua Uruguaiana 174, Centro, tel. 021/2509–6017). **Riotur** (Rua da Assembléia 10, near Praça 15 de Novembro, Centro, tel. 021/2217–7575). **Riotur information booth** (Av. Princesa Isabel 183 Copacabana, tel. 021/2541–7522). **Turisrio** (Rua da Assembléia 10, 7th and 8th floors, Centro, tel. 021/2531–1922).

➤ **U.S. GOVERNMENT ADVISORIES: U.S. Department of State** (Overseas Citizens Services Office, Room 4811 N.S., 2201 C St. NW, Washington, DC 20520, tel. 202/647–5225 for interactive hot line, http://travel.state.gov/travel/html); enclose a self-addressed, stamped, business-size envelope.

Web Sites

Do check out the World Wide Web when planning your trip. You'll find everything from weather forecasts to virtual tours of famous cities. Be sure to **visit Fodors.com** (www.fodors.com), a complete travel-planning site. You can research prices and book plane tickets, hotel rooms, rental cars, vacation packages, and more. In addition, you can post your pressing questions in the Travel Talk section. Other planning tools include a currency converter and weather reports, and there are loads of links to travel resources.

Don't rule out foreign-language sites; some have links to sites that present information in more than one language, including English. On Portuguese-language sites, watch for the name of the region, state, or city in which you have an interest.

The following sites should get you started: www.embratur.gov.br (the official Brazilian tourist board site, with information in English provided by the Brazilian embassy in London), www.varig.com (Varig Airlines's site, with English information), www.brazilny.org (the official consular Web site in New York, with details about other consulates and the embassy as well as travel information and links to other sites), www.brazilinfocenter.org (a Washington, D.C.–based organization that promotes political and business issues, rather than tourism, but whose Web site has an incredible number of helpful links), www.vivabrazil.com (a site with background and travel info on Brazil's different regions as well as links that will help you arrange your trip).

When to Go

CLIMATE

Seasons below the equator are the reverse of the north—summer in Brazil runs from December to March and winter from June to September. The rainy season in Brazil occurs during the summer months, but this is rarely a nuisance. Showers can be torrential but usually last no more than an hour or two.

Prices in beach resorts are invariably higher during the high season (Brazilian summer). If you're looking for a bargain, stick to the off-season (May–June and August–October; July is school-break month). In Rio and at beach resorts along the coast, especially in the northeast, these months offer the added attraction of relief from the often oppressive summer heat, although in Rio the temperature can drop to uncomfortable levels for swimming in June through August.

Rio de Janeiro is on the tropic of Capricorn, and its climate is just that—tropical. Summers are hot and humid, with temperatures rising as high as 105°F (40°C), although the average ranges between 84°F and 95°F (29°C–35°C). In winter, temperatures stay in the 70s (20s C), occasionally dipping into the high 60s (15°C–20°C).

➤ **FORECASTS: Weather Channel Connection** (tel. 900/932–8437), 95¢ per minute from a Touch-Tone phone.

The following are the average daily maximum and minimum temperatures for Rio de Janeiro.

Jan.	84F	29C	**May**	77F	25C	**Sept.**	75F	24C
	69	21		66	19		66	19
Feb.	85F	29C	**June**	76F	24C	**Oct.**	77F	25C
	73	23		64	18		63	17
Mar.	83F	28C	**July**	75F	24C	**Nov.**	79F	26C
	72	22		64	18		68	20
Apr.	80F	27C	**Aug.**	76F	24C	**Dec.**	82F	28C
	69	21		64	18		71	22

WORDS AND PHRASES

Basics

English	Portuguese	Pronunciation
Yes/no	Sim/Não	**seeing**/**nown**
Please	Por favor	pohr fah-**vohr**
May I?	Posso?	**poh**-sso
Thank you (very much)	(Muito) obrigado	(**mooyn**-too) o-bree **gah**-doh
You're welcome	De nada	day **nah**-dah
Excuse me	Com licença	con lee-**ssehn**-ssah
Pardon me/what did you say?	Desculpe/O que disse?	des-**kool**-peh/o.k. **dih**-say?
Could you tell me?	Poderia me dizer?	po-day-**ree**-ah mee dee-**zehrr**?
I'm sorry	Sinto muito	**seen**-too **mooyn**-too
Good morning!	Bom dia!	bohn **dee**-ah
Good afternoon!	Boa tarde!	**boh**-ah **tahr**-dee
Good evening!	Boa noite!	**boh**-ah **nohee-tee**
Goodbye!	Adeus!/Até logo!	ah-**dehoos**/ah-**teh** **loh**-go
Mr./Mrs.	Senhor/Senhora	sen-**yor**/sen-**yohr**-ah
Miss	Senhorita	sen-yo-**ri**-tah
Pleased to meet you	Muito prazer	**mooyn**-too prah-**zehr**
How are you?	Como vai?	**koh**-mo **vah**-ee
Very well, thank you	Muito bem, obrigado	**mooyn**-too **beh**-in o-bree-**gah**-doh
And you?	E o(a) Senhor(a)?	eh oh sen-**yor** (**yohr**-ah)
Hello (on the telephone)	Alô	ah-**low**

Numbers

1	um/uma	oom/**oom**-ah
2	dois	**dohees**
3	três	**trehys**
4	quatro	**kwa**-troh
5	cinco	**seen**-koh
6	seis	**sehys**
7	sete	**seh**-tee
8	oito	**ohee**-too
9	nove	**noh**-vee
10	dez	**deh**-ees
11	onze	**ohn**-zee
12	doze	**doh**-zee
13	treze	**treh**-zee
14	quatorze	kwa-**tohr**-zee
15	quinze	**keen**-zee
16	dezesseis	deh-zeh-**sehys**
17	dezessete	deh-zeh-**seh**-tee
18	dezoito	deh-**zohee**-toh
19	dezenove	deh-zeh-**noh**-vee
20	vinte	**veen**-tee
21	vinte e um	**veen**-tee eh **oom**
30	trinta	**treen**-tah
40	quarenta	kwa-**rehn**-ta
50	cinquenta	seen-**kwehn**-tah
60	sessenta	seh-**sehn**-tah
70	setenta	seh-**tehn**-tah
80	oitenta	ohee-**tehn**-ta
90	noventa	noh-**vehn**-ta
100	cem	**seh**-ing
101	cento e um	**sehn**-too e **oom**
200	duzentos	doo-**zehn**-tohss
500	quinhentos	key-**nyehn**-tohss
700	setecentos	seh-teh-**sehn**-tohss
900	novecentos	noh-veh-**sehn**-tohss
1,000	mil	meel
2,000	dois mil	**dohees** meel
1,000,000	um milhão	oom mee-lee-**ahon**

Days of the Week

Sunday	Domingo	doh-**meehn**-goh
Monday	Segunda-feira	seh-**goon**-dah **fey**-rah
Tuesday	Terça-feira	**tehr**-sah **fey**-rah
Wednesday	Quarta-feira	**kwahr**-tah **fey**-rah
Thursday	Quinta-feira	**keen**-tah **fey**-rah
Friday	Sexta-feira	**sehss**-tah **fey**-rah
Saturday	Sábado	**sah**-bah-doh

Useful Phrases

Do you speak English?	O Senhor fala inglês?	oh sen-**yor fah**-lah een-**glehs**?
I don't speak Portuguese.	Não falo português.	nown **fah**-loh pohr-too-**ghehs**
I don't understand (you)	Não lhe entendo	nown lyeh ehn-**tehn**-doh
I understand	Eu entendo	**eh**-oo ehn-**tehn**-doh
I don't know	Não sei	nown say
I am American/ British	Sou americano (americana)/ inglês/inglêsa	sow a-meh-ree-**cah**-noh (a-meh-ree-**cah**-nah/ een-**glehs**(een-**glah**-sa)
What's your name?	Como se chama?	**koh**-moh seh **shah**-mah
My name is . . .	Meu nome é . . .	mehw **noh**-meh eh
What time is it?	Que horas são?	keh **oh**-rahss **sa**-ohn
It is one, two, three . . . o'clock	É uma/São duas, três . . . hora/horas	eh **oom**-ah/**sa**-ohn **oomah**, **doo**-ahss, **trehys oh**-rah/**oh**-rahs
Yes, please/No, thank you	Sim por favor/ Não obrigado	seing pohr fah-**vohr**/ nown o-bree-**gah**-doh
How?	Como?	**koh**-moh
When?	Quando?	**kwahn**-doh
This/Next week	Esta/Próxima semana	**ehss**-tah/**proh**-see-mah seh-**mah**-nah
This/Next month	Este/Próximo mêz	**ehss**-teh/**proh**-see-moh mehz
This/Next year	Este/Próximo ano	**ehss**-teh/**proh**-see-moh **ah**-noh

Yesterday/today tomorrow	Ontem/hoje amanhã	**ohn**-tehn/**oh**-jeh/ ah-mah-**nyan**
This morning/ afternoon	Esta manhã/ tarde	**ehss**-tah mah-**nyan** / **tahr**-deh
Tonight	Hoje a noite	**oh**-jeh ah **nohee**-tee
What?	O que?	oh **keh**
What is it?	O que é isso?	oh **keh** eh **ee**-soh
Why?	Por quê?	pohr-**keh**
Who?	Quem?	**keh**-in
Where is . . . ?	Onde é . . . ?	**ohn**-deh **eh**
the train station?	a estação de trem?	ah es-tah-**sah**-on deh train
the subway station?	a estação de metrô?	ah es-tah-**sah**-on deh meh-**tro**
the bus stop?	a parada do ônibus?	ah pah-**rah**-dah doh **oh**-nee-boos
the post office?	o correio?	oh coh-**hay**-yoh
the bank?	o banco?	oh **bahn**-koh
the hotel?	o hotel . . . ?	oh oh-**tell**
the cashier?	o caixa?	oh **kahy**-shah
the museum?	o museo . . . ?	oh moo-**zeh**-oh
the hospital?	o hospital?	oh ohss-pee-**tal**
the elevator?	o elevador?	oh eh-leh-vah-**dohr**
the bathroom?	o banheiro?	oh bahn-**yey**-roh
the beach?	a praia de . . . ?	ah **prahy**-yah deh
Here/there	Aqui/ali	ah-**kee**/ah-**lee**
Open/closed	Aberto/fechado	ah-**behr**-toh/feh-**shah**-doh
Left/right	Esquerda/ direita	ehs-**kehr**-dah/ dee-**ray**-tah
Straight ahead	Em frente	ehyn **frehn**-teh
Is it near/far?	É perto/longe?	eh **pehr**-toh/**lohn**-jeh
I'd like to buy . . .	Gostaria de comprar . . .	gohs-tah-**ree**-ah deh cohm-**prahr** . . .
a map	um mapa	oom **mah**-pah
suntan lotion bronzear	um óleo de brohn-zeh-**ahr**	oom **oh**-lyoh deh

a ticket	um bilhete	oom bee-**lyeh**-teh
cigarettes	cigarros	see-**gah**-hose
envelopes	envelopes	eyn-veh-**loh**-pehs
matches	fósforos	**fohs**-foh-rohss
paper	papel	pah-**pehl**
sandals	sandália	sahn-**dah**-leeah
soap	sabonete	sah-bow-**neh**-teh
How much is it?	Quanto custa?	**kwahn**-too **koos**-tah
It's expensive/ cheap	Está caro/ barato	ehss-**tah kah**-roh / bah-**rah**-toh
A little/a lot	Um pouco/muito	oom **pohw**-koh/ **moo**yn-too
More/less	Mais/menos	**mah**-ees /**meh**-nohss
Enough/too much/too little	Suficiente/ demais/ muito pouco	soo-fee-see-**ehn**-teh/ deh-**mah**-ees/ **moo**yn-toh **pohw**-koh
Telephone	Telefone	teh-leh-**foh**-neh
Telegram	Telegrama	teh-leh-**grah**-mah
I am ill.	Estou doente.	ehss-**tow** doh-**ehn**-teh
Please call a doctor.	Por favor chame um médico.	pohr fah-**vohr shah**-meh oom **meh**-dee-koh
Help!	Socorro!	soh-**koh**-ho
Help me!	Me ajude!	mee ah-**jyew**-deh
Fire!	Incêndio!	een-**sehn**-deeoh
Caution!/Look out!/ Be careful!	Cuidado!	kooy-**dah**-doh

Dining Out

A bottle of . . .	Uma garrafa de . . .	**oo**mah gah-**hah**-fah deh
A cup of . . .	Uma xícara de . . .	**oo**mah **shee**-kah-rah deh
A glass of . . .	Um copo de . . .	oom **koh**-poh deh
Ashtray	Um cinzeiro	oom seen-**zeh**y-roh
Bill/check	A conta	ah **kohn**-tah
Bread	Pão	**pah**-on
Breakfast	Café da manhã	kah-**feh** dah mah-**nyan**

Butter	A manteiga	ah mahn-**tehy**-gah
Cheers!	Saúde!	sah-**oo**-deh
Cocktail	Um aperitivo	oom ah-peh-ree-**tee**-voh
Dinner	O jantar	oh **jyahn**-tahr
Dish	Um prato	oom **prah**-toh
Enjoy!	Bom apetite!	bohm ah-peh-**tee**-teh
Fork	Um garfo	**gahr**-foh
Fruit	Fruta	**froo**-tah
Is the tip included?	A gorjeta esta incluída?	ah gohr-**jyeh**-tah ehss-**tah** een-clue-**ee**-dah
Juice	Um suco	oom **soo**-koh
Knife	Uma faca	**oo**mah **fah**-kah
Lunch	O almoço	oh ahl-**moh**-ssoh
Menu	Menu/cardápio	me-**noo** /kahr-**dah**-peeoh
Mineral water	Água mineral	**ah**-gooah mee-neh-**rahl**
Napkin	Guardanapo	gooahr-dah-**nah**-poh
(No) smoking	(Não) fumante	nown foo-**mahn**-teh
Pepper	Pimenta	pee-**mehn**-tah
Please give me	Por favor me dê	pohr fah-**vohr** mee **deh**
Salt	Sal	sahl
Spoon	Uma colher	**oo**mah koh-**lyehr**
Sugar	Açúcar	ah-**soo**-kahr
Waiter!	Garçon!	gahr-**sohn**
Water	Água	**ah**-gooah
Wine	Vinho	**vee**-nyoh

index

ICONS AND SYMBOLS

★ Our special recommendations
Good for kids (rubber duck)
③ ❸ Numbers in white and black circles that appear on the maps, in the margins, and within the tours correspond to one another.

Your checklist for a perfect journey

WAY AHEAD

- Devise a trip budget.
- Write down the five things you want most from this trip. Keep this list handy before and during your trip.
- Make plane or train reservations. Book lodging and rental cars.
- Arrange for pet care.
- Check your passport. Apply for a new one if necessary.
- Photocopy important documents and store in a safe place.

A MONTH BEFORE

- Make restaurant reservations and buy theater and concert tickets. Visit fodors.com for links to local events.
- Familiarize yourself with the local language or lingo.

TWO WEEKS BEFORE

- Replenish your supply of medications.
- Create your itinerary.
- Enjoy a book or movie set in your destination to get you in the mood.
- Develop a packing list. Shop for missing essentials. Repair and launder or dry-clean your clothes.

A WEEK BEFORE

- Stop newspaper deliveries. Pay bills.
- Acquire traveler's checks.
- Stock up on film.
- Label your luggage.
- Finalize your packing list—take less than you think you need.
- Create a toiletries kit filled with travel-size essentials.
- Get lots of sleep. Don't get sick before your trip.

A DAY BEFORE

- Drink plenty of water.
- Check your travel documents.
- Get packing!

DURING YOUR TRIP

- Keep a journal/scrapbook.
- Spend time with locals.
- Take time to explore. Don't plan too much.

Distance Conversion Chart

Kilometers/Miles

To change kilometers (km) to miles (mi), multiply km by .621.
To change mi to km, multiply mi by 1.61.

km to mi	mi to km
1 = .62	1 = 1.6
2 = 1.2	2 = 3.2
3 = 1.9	3 = 4.8
4 = 2.5	4 = 6.4
5 = 3.1	5 = 8.1
6 = 3.7	6 = 9.7
7 = 4.3	7 = 11.3
8 = 5.0	8 = 12.9

Meters/Feet

To change meters (m) to feet (ft), multiply m by 3.28.
To change ft to m, multiply ft by .305.

m to ft	ft to m
1 = 3.3	1 = .30
2 = 6.6	2 = .61
3 = 9.8	3 = .92
4 = 13.1	4 = 1.2
5 = 16.4	5 = 1.5
6 = 19.7	6 = 1.8
7 = 23.0	7 = 2.1
8 = 26.2	8 = 2.4

FODOR'S POCKET RIO DE JANEIRO

EDITORS: Carissa Bluestone, Laura M. Kidder

Editorial Contributors: Joyce Dalton, Denise Garcia, Ana Lúcia do Vale

Editorial Production: Marina Padakis

Maps: David Lindroth, *cartographer;* Bob Blake and Rebecca Baer, *map editors*

Design: Fabrizio La Rocca, *creative director;* Tigist Getachew, *art director;* Melanie Marin, *photo editor*

Production/Manufacturing: Colleen Ziemba

Cover Photo: Darius Koehli/ Age Fotostock

COPYRIGHT

 Published in the United States by Fodor's Travel Publications, a unit of Fodors LLC, a subsidiary of Random House, Inc., and simultaneously in Canada by Random House of Canada, Limited, Toronto. Distributed by Random House, Inc., New York.

Second Edition

ISBN 0-676-90193-X

ISSN 1527-6287

IMPORTANT TIP

Although all prices, opening times, and other details in this book are based on information supplied to us at press time, changes occur all the time in the travel world, and Fodor's cannot accept responsibility for facts that become outdated or for inadvertent errors or omissions. So **always confirm information when it matters,** especially if you're making a detour to visit a specific place.

SPECIAL SALES

Fodor's Travel Publications are available at special discounts for bulk purchases for sales promotions or premiums. Special editions, including personalized covers, excerpts of existing guides, and corporate imprints, can be created in large quantities for special needs. For more information, contact your local bookseller or write to Special Markets, Fodor's Travel Publications, 280 Park Avenue, New York, NY 10017. Inquiries from Canada should be directed to your local Canadian bookseller or sent to Random House of Canada, Ltd., Marketing Department, 2775 Matheson Boulevard East, Mississauga, Ontario L4W 4P7. Inquiries from the United Kingdom should be sent to Fodor's Travel Publications, 20 Vauxhall Bridge Road, London SW1V 2SA, England.

PRINTED IN THE UNITED STATES OF AMERICA

10 9 8 7 6 5 4 3 2 1